TO:

FROM:

DATE:

From Prayer to WARFARE

Ana G. Maldonado

Our Vision

To take the Word of God everywhere it is needed
and to spiritually feed God's people through
preaching, teaching, and books.

From Prayer To Warfare

First Edition 2005

ISBN: 1-59272-179-6

Cover Design by:
ERJ Publications – Design Department

Category:
Intercession and Spiritual Warfare

Published by:
ERJ Publications
14291 SW 142 St., Miami, FL 33186
(305) 233-3325 – Fax: (305) 233-3328

Printed in Colombia

DEDICATION

This book is dedicated to the author and finisher of our faith, our Lord Jesus Christ; and, to the Holy Spirit, who taught me how to pray effectively and for promoting me from prayer into intercession and warfare. Also, I want to dedicate this book to the early-morning prayer warriors who dare to conquer territories in order to enthrone God's name; they are not afraid to face the enemy in warfare to achieve their objectives.

May God's grace and favor always be with you!

ACKNOWLEDGEMENTS

Sometimes, God places in our lives people with the ability to change us forever. Ligia Lacayo is such a person. God blessed my life with her friendship during difficult moments at the beginning of this ministry, and for that, I am eternally grateful. She was a role model of faithfulness, support, and of what it means to be a pillar of prayer and intercession.

Also, I would like to express my appreciation to the intercessors that take their place in the gap, day and night, to protect and sustain the hedge of protection around this ministry; they have fully understood that we live in a time of warfare from which we cannot surrender.

INDEX

PROLOGUE

We were created by God with purpose and potential, but these are often hindered by different situations that prevent them from becoming a reality. We must learn to take a stand and fight to achieve our goals. We must do everything that is within our power to make certain that God's plan for our lives is accomplished. When we see the purpose and will of God for our lives developing, we will achieve a level of personal satisfaction as individuals. For this reason, I admire my wife; she is a prayer warrior who knows how to fight until the job gets done. Through prayer and spiritual warfare, she obtains God's blessings, directions, and purpose that need to be applied to the ministry and our personal lives. This is not an easy task to accomplish — before any objective is successfully completed, there is a war that must be fought in the Spirit. Everyday, rain or shine, my wife walks towards her destiny through prayer; her determination opens the doors that lead to the victory that we freely enjoy today.

The Lord has prepared great blessings for His children, but adversity and hardship causes them to question how they will receive the blessings that God intends to place in their hands. However, if they believe that God wants to bless them, and if they were to take a decisive action upon that belief and make war for it until they see a breakthrough, they would stop the enemy from taking their blessings and finally be able to enjoy them.

In this book, through my wife's testimony and experiences, you will find clear examples of perseverance that will encourage you to fight for the dreams that God has placed in your heart. In your determination to follow God's direction, you might have to experience hard times, but do not give up. God will stand by your side as He has done for my wife. During moments of crisis when she found herself surrounded by the reality of a harsh and unkind world, my wife found refuge and direction through prayer and warfare; her closeness to God strengthened her to continue in her quest and to accomplish His will for her life. God never makes a mistake! God does not see who we are right now; He sees the final product — what we will become. If we want God's purpose and will to manifest in our lives, then we must learn to see through God's eyes; His vision for us will be the hand that guides our path to victory.

Guillermo Maldonado
Pastor

INTRODUCTION

The reason I wrote this book is because I want my experiences to serve as a tool and a guiding light to every person who reads it. My prayer for you today is that you may be touched by what you read; may it serve as an inspiration, a blessing, and a revelation of the true meaning of prayer. May you be strengthened by this message and encouraged to rise up and begin to take charge of your life and ministry through the practice of effective spiritual warfare against the enemy.

Before writing this book, I hesitated about the project. I kept asking myself, "Why should I write a book if my husband is the author in the family?" Not only is he an excellent writer, but he is also an excellent pastor, teacher, father, husband, and friend. I admire him greatly because I see how God uses him, not only in his preaching but also through his books. I decided to share my testimony with you because I want to encourage you not to give up. I want you to see what God can do for you — He can sweep you into His loving arms, touch your heart, confront, and encourage you to stop the complaining and bickering. He will guide your steps towards becoming a powerful child of God — one who is capable of successfully achieving that which God has called you to do.

Our prayers can change the destiny of our lives. I am certain that El Rey Jesus International Ministry would not be what it is today had we not paid the price in prayer. Today, I rejoice in the fact that the heavens are open over our ministry. It is not because of one person but because of God's grace and favor and the power of prayer; our church has implemented the 24 hours a day prayer ministry. Prayer manifests the will of God in powerful ways. I have witnessed the power of prayer manifest at home, in my family, and at church. The power of prayer and warfare is the fuel that ignites the fire of revival in our churches, our families, and in us.

At the end of this book, you will read the testimonies of several men whose lives have been transformed by the power of prayer. Some may ask why I chose to include testimonies of men and not women. The answer is simple. I want to encourage men to pray. Unfortunately, many people today are still in spiritual bondage; they are held back by their beliefs. Strongholds and paradigms overshadow their understanding making them believe that women are the only people who should fast and pray. This mentality causes men to stand back and not exercise the authority that they have as the representatives of the priesthood of Jesus Christ in the home. Unfortunately, the position of priesthood has deteriorated rapidly; men are not taking their place as head of their homes. God has placed in my heart a burden for these men. I am constantly crying out to God to raise men who are willing to pray. I constantly challenge men to take their rightful place as priests, as head of their homes, and as part of the ministry team together with their wives. Also, I encourage men not to view the word "submission" as male domination, but rather, to understand that submission from their wives is the direct result of their love for them. Wives will submit to men who pray and who are good role models. For instance, a wife will submit to her husband when he learns to love her in the same way that Jesus loves women: with kindness and gentleness.

Men must be encouraged and motivated to seek God; they must take the initiative and become what God wants them to be. Of course, women must continue to seek God, but we need to see men who are role models in today's society — real men, as God created them to be from the beginning.

A man who prays, who reads the Word, and who gives a good testimony of what he preaches and teaches is followed by his wife, children, and peers. It is a pleasure for a wife to submit to her husband when he seeks God wholeheartedly. On the other hand, if a husband is not a good role model to his family, his wife should continue to pray for him; a husband's lack of desire for the things of God is not an excuse to give up. If a husband does not like to pray, his wife must become the prayer warrior; she should stand in the gap for her husband and repair the breach that will lead to his change of attitude; she should never give up regardless of his attitude, mentality, or behavior. A wife who knows how to persevere in prayer and spiritual warfare can lead her husband to church, to pray, and to serve in ministry. The prayer of a righteous person triumphs over adversity. Prayer causes the will of God to take action; it pulls every virtue and gift of God into existence, including: His gift of love, salvation, deliverance, healing, and much more. When we pray, we take what God has, and is, and we bring it home; we establish it in our lives, our citiest, and nations.

I pray that you may receive the impartation, the desire, and the realization of the need for prayer. May your level of relationship, spiritual maturity, and communion with the Lord increase more each day.

I declare that this book will be a great blessing to you. Again, I want to express my gratitude to the Lord — my beloved Jesus, the only One who is worthy of the glory, the honor, the power, and the Lordship.

CHAPTER I

THE EARLY YEARS

"⁴As for your nativity, on the day you were born your navel cord was not cut, nor were you washed in water to cleanse you; you were not rubbed with salt nor wrapped in swaddling cloths. ⁵No eye pitied you, to do any of these things for you, to have compassion on you; but you were thrown out into the open field, when you yourself were loathed on the day you were born. ⁶And when I passed by you and saw you struggling in your own blood, I said to you in your blood, 'Live!' Yes, I said to you in your blood, 'Live'." Ezekiel 16.4-6

I cannot deny the fact that I am in this world thanks to the powerful and merciful hand of the Lord! On August 22, 1963, I came into this world by a miracle of God. I can say this because I know for certain that my mother did not want me to be born; she tried on three different occasions to terminate the pregnancy; after seven children, it was hard for her to accept the fact that another child was on the way. Though she tried to end my life, I did become her favorite child. I know this because she told my brothers and sisters that I was the quietest, the one who worked the hardest, the most intelligent, and the one with leadership qualities that were above the rest of her children. She noticed that I had the ability to lead the rest and that is why she and I got along very well.

Now I realize that it was the devil — not my mother — that tried to destroy my life from the moment I entered her womb. The devil's plan to destroy me failed because the powerful hand of the Lord was there to shelter me, protect me, cover me, and give me life. God chose me; He pointed me out and separated me since before the foundation of the world.

As I look at my life, family, and ministry, it is easy to understand why I had to experience the things that I had to overcome. It is the realization of this truth that encourages me to share my testimony with you today. I want it to be an inspiration to you and to everyone who thinks that they are incapable of doing great things. I want to give you the confidence to go forward and to inspire you to fulfill the purpose and destiny of God for your lives. I want to unmask the enemy by informing you that the devil has not defeated you; he has not won. I say this to you because the devil thought he could destroy me, but the devil does not have the last word. My life might have started in hardship but God has glorified Himself in my life; He overturned the evil that was intended to destroy my life and created a renewing, restoring, and amazing miracle in me. If He did it for me, He can also do it for you!

The Early Years

Let us return to August 22, 1963. The day I was born, my parents and seven brothers and sisters were living in a small town called "La Joya" which is located in Santander, Colombia. The area surrounding this town is called "El Peñon" because of the large boulders and stones that decorate the land; some of these great rocks are the size of buildings that measure twenty floors high. The soil in this part of the country was so rich that any seed that was planted brought forth fruit. We lived in this beautiful land where my father lovingly built a home for his family; the view from our house was breathtaking; everywhere we looked the mountains were there to embrace our beautiful home. The house was built with a master bedroom for my parents and a very large room that I shared with my fifteen brothers and sisters. This may not seem like a big and spacious house, but to our family it was. I am the eighth daughter of Anibal Duarte and Leonilde Vargas. My brothers and sisters are: Samuel, Ines, Rito (1), Ana Bertilia (1), Rito (2), Misael, Florentino, Lucia, Maria Jesus, Ana Bertilia (2), Marlene, Eduardo, Rito (3), and Ana Licenia. I know what you are thinking, but to this day, I have no idea why mom named so many of us Rito and Ana, but I figure she had her reasons.

In this book, I will share with you a few experiences from my life. Let me begin my story by saying that my childhood was very different than that of children today. One of the earliest memories that I can recall while growing up in La Joya happened when I was a four year old little girl. This memory is very vivid in my mind; it changed me forever. One day I walked into my house and heard my mother crying; it was not an ordinary cry, but a cry that made me suddenly realize that she was about to have her next child. The shock of seeing mom in labor and witnessing the effects of childbirth traumatized me. To see a live birth at any age can be an incredible experience, but for a four year old to witness her mom giving birth, in the condition that she did, was far too disturbing for me. Nevertheless, in 1967, in a house hidden by the mountains, mom gave birth — alone. Talk about an eye-opening experience! I learned early on that when mom purchased a rope it was because her time to deliver the baby was near. This might be hard to explain and even harder to imagine, but she would wrap the rope on the strongest and highest beam in the house and used it to help her get through each contraction; somehow, the rope replaced the helping hands that are readily available to women who are about to deliver their babies today. I remember mom's endless suffering during the delivery process. The babies were usually not in a rush to be born, and so, she had to endure many days of pain; her crying and screaming was heard throughout the house.

When mom was not delivering her next child, our days consisted in waking up before dawn — three or four in the morning — to work the land, help mom raise her children, and do what was needed around the house; this was a lot of work. As a small child who had to work so much, it was hard for me to obey; after all, it is not an easy thing to get up at three o'clock in the morning, especially for a child who knew that the dawn of a new day only promised that more work needed to be done. On the days that I woke up with this "uncooperative" attitude, mom would punish me severely; she did not spare the rod. Her words of wisdom were: "You will learn to obey the easy way or the hard way. If you choose the hard way, I will teach you with the rod; either way, you will learn to obey."

My mother's rule for discipline inspired me to obey and to complete my daily chores which seemed to go on forever; there was always one more thing that needed to be done. Once the work for the day was completed, the day was also over and it was time for bed. This was our daily routine from dawn to sundown: work, work, and more work — it takes a lot of manpower to run such a large household. In my house, there were always at least four children at home, one right after the other in age that needed to be taken care of — mom would get pregnant with the next child almost immediately after delivery (My fifteen brothers and sisters are less than a year apart in age).

I took care of children throughout my entire childhood; I practically raised my brothers and sisters, though I was a child that needed to be raised herself. In truth, I can say that I had no childhood. I saw and experienced things that no child should have to live through. If you were to ask me to share with you one positive thing that came out of this life of hardship, I would have to say that my experiences taught me to work hard and honestly. Praise God for that! I learned to make wise decisions and to deal with any situation that was thrown at me; I learned to plow the land, plant the seed, and collect the harvest; I worked very hard on those mountains to help feed my family. Looking back, I know that those years of hard work were the training ground for who I am today. If we want something in life, we have to work hard for it. If it is worth having, it is worth fighting for!

Moving on, have you ever heard that a person can feel alone while standing in the middle of a crowd? I am the example of such a person. Al though I was constantly surrounded by children and people, I still felt very alone. Yes, I had a mother that was physically there but who was also too busy to notice that I needed her; she was always preocupied with my brothers and sisters, pregnant, working, and suffering. I also had a father, but he was rarely with us because he was always working the land in towns that were eight hours away from home. In those days, distances were traveled on foot because cars, carriages, or horses were luxuries that we could not afford. I felt alone and abandoned.

My mother never offered words of affirmation or love; I do not recall her ever taking time to say a positive word of encouragement. I do not remember her ever hugging or physically expressing love to me or any of the other children. My siblings could not be counted upon to provide the love that I desperately needed because they were also in need of love. I remember that when they reached the age of twelve or thirteen they would pack what few possessions they had and left home in search for a new life — they dared to dream for a better future. Once they left, we rarely saw them again. My eldest sister is one who chose to leave and not look back; we never saw or heard from her again.

Having her children leave home at such a young age must have caused mom terrible pain and heartache, but this was not her only source of pain. She had too many questions concerning the events in her life that demanded explanations that never arrived; she had too many children that demanded her attention; too much work with no end in sight, too many wants and needs that she could not satisfy, and too many people around her that she had to defend us from.

One thing I could count on while growing up was to hear mom constantly complain about being a woman; she was quick to express her feelings on this subject. She wished she had been born a man; according to her, men did not suffer as much as women. She said that to be born female was a curse that guaranteed hard work, suffering, and labor pains. Mom always looked sad and unhappy. There was always a tear ready to roll down her cheeks. Not only was she emotionally distressed but she was also physically worn out; she suffered serious blood loss almost every month which caused her to feel weak and ill. Her constant complaining about how hard it was to be a woman, her bitterness, and frustration started to contaminate my young heart.

While I cannot deny that growing up in La Joya was hard, I also cannot deny that we were extremely blessed by God. We were the only people in the area with natural water springs; they kept us from suffering the effects of the drought in the dry season.

Other people were not so blessed, for they could not enjoy this benefit. Our good fortune awakened the envy in some of our neighbors who often tried to take advantage of our lands and water springs. When the men from other lands came to steal what we had, my mother would confront them; she fearlessly defended what was ours and used every ounce of strength to protect us. I saw her fight many times; often, she was beaten so hard that we thought she had fought her last fight. I witnessed my mother, all too often, near the edge of death because of her strong character. She was called the "Lioness" because she was always predisposed to fight and to give up her life to protect what was hers. My brothers, sisters, and I would join these fights to try and help our mother, but the men were stronger than us; we suffered terrible beatings at the mercy of these dreadful men. I recall that my arm was broken during one of these fights, but we fought back and never surrendered. Praise God there were never any casualties, but the fighting, the blood, and the dreaded feeling that someday someone was going to kill my mother overwhelmed my young mind. These were horrible times!

While mom defended our properties, my dad worked the land — it was not easy trying to feed a family with eighteen mouths. Everybody had to work. In fact, the amount of work that we had to do was so great that it left room for nothing else, not even school. I loved going to school, but I was unable to attend because of my daily schedule of work. I remember that I would attend school one week and miss the next. My attendance record made it difficult for me to learn. The teachers, instead of understanding my predicament, would hit me out of frustration; I suppose they thought that this method of "beat the child" would improve my learning skills — they did not.

I remember as if this happened yesterday, the day that one of those teachers grabbed me and started to slap my face. Needless to say, this was not what I needed at the time. Between my mother's complaining and suffering, between the hard work and the feeling of abandonment, between the abuse at school and the frustration of not being able to learn, the bitterness and resentment that my mother had planted into my spirit began to grow deeper inside of me.

The early years of my life hold very painful memories. These were also years that lacked abundance and material possessions. I owned my first pair of shoes when I was eleven years old, and I only owned one dress — my beloved red dress!

The Red Dress...

I know this is hard to believe, but I only owned one piece of clothing — my beloved red dress. One vivid memory that stands out among the rest is the walk I had to take everyday down to the river to wash diapers. I remember it vividly. Every time I went to the river, I encountered a ferocious bull that always seemed eager to come after me. Each time he saw me, he dashed after me. Remember, I was a seven year old child who "had" to wear the red dress because it was the only piece of clothing I owned. I did not know that bulls are attracted by the color red or by running children. In my young mind, this beast was not a bull chewing grass, but a demon that wanted to destroy me. Now, when I remember those days, I laugh, but at the time it was not funny; it was terrifying.

My "red dress bull experience" took the joy out of washing diapers, but the memories do not end there. Some time after my eighth birthday, my red dress got very dirty while planting corn. I knew what my mother would say if she were to see me dirty, so I quickly took off my dress, washed it, and hanged it to dry near the wood stove. I was hoping that it would dry before the farmers (about 100 men) arrived for the meal break. Things did not go as I planned. While waiting in the attic of the house for the dress to dry, I noticed that the workers were beginning to arrive. Can you picture this? There I am, eight years old, naked, and literally nailed to the floor. My shame was so great that I did not know what to do. When I finally decided to move, I did the only thing a little girl can do; I ran to my mother's arms hoping that she would cover my nakedness. To my surprise, instead of embracing me in her protective arms, she froze and started to laugh. Though this might seem like a funny story to you, it was not funny to me. That particular moment stayed with me for a very long time; it made me feel even more alone than ever. I was a little girl in need of her mother's protection which I did not receive. Her lack of action was extremely hard for me to forgive.

Another moment lived in my red dress was the day my brother Misael and I were cooking soup — I do not recall what kind — and my younger brother Elasio (only four years old) tried to serve himself from the steaming pot. Picture this, a four year old next to a large pot filled with steaming soup enough to feed at least 18 people. Please remember that this pot was not on a stove too high for a small child to reach. Instead, this pot was on the ground and within his reach. His hunger overshadowed his sense of survival. In his attempt to serve the soup, he fell into the pot and its steaming contents. Misael and I managed to pull Elasio out of the pot, but the soup had done damage; his burns were impressive. As you can imagine, Misael and I were petrified that mom was going to kill us for not watching Elasio and so we did the only thing our young minds could come up with: We poured water on Elasio and ran – we ran into the mountains until there was no more breath left in our lungs. We were terrified!

I wish all of my "red dress" moments were as funny as the bull by the river or even as harmless as the attic experience, but they were not. I lived other moments in my red dress — like the one with Elasio and the soup or the one that I am about to share with you — these were extremely painful. Remembering my red dress also reminds me of the time that I witnessed the rape of my younger sister. This is a horrific moment that has been engraved forever in the pages of my personal history. As I recall, my sister and I were out in the field, and for a moment, we were separated. When I heard unfamiliar noises, I hid behind some rocks because I was afraid. I was careful to look around trying to discover where the noise was coming from. Suddenly, my eyes focused on the men and my younger sister. My body froze in terror as I watched these men hold her down against her will and rape her — she had not celebrated her 10th birthday. The shock of what I saw scarred me forever.

Questions without answers began to pound my young mind. One of these questions repeated itself over and over again, "Why?" This "why" was more than a question; it was a cry of frustration, pain, and anger; it was the "why" that made me feel like breaking something. The minutes seemed like an eternity. I hid behind those rocks unable to move; I was terrified to leave my shelter because I was afraid that if I tried to defend my sister, these men would do the same to me. As I watched in horror, I desperately tried to make sense of what was happening, but I could not. I hid my face and thought to myself, "Is this what life is all about?" Yet, something inside of me kept telling me that this was wrong, it was "not normal". Like I said, I was young. I did not understand everything; I was still in the learning process of what was real or not. At home, we were never exposed to topics of conversation that went beyond the events of the day. We heard discussions about land, seeds, water, animals, among others, but we were never exposed nor did anyone take the time to explain to the little kids the evil intentions that hide in the hearts of men. We were kept naive on the "forbidden subjects", yet, if we had been properly made aware of certain dangers, perhaps what happened to my sister would never have happened.

Now that I think about it, it is kind of ironic that while growing up, we saw our mother beat men up with her bare hands when they tried to come against us or threaten to rape us. Yet, neither her heart nor her intuition as a woman enlightened her as to what happened and continued to happen to her little girl; she was completely in the dark about it. I could have said something, but I did not. I was afraid that if I opened my mouth to say anything, my mother would kill my sister for "allowing it" and the men for raping her — I kept quiet.

At this point, you might be curious to find out a little more about this event, but I am purposely omitting a few details and the names of the men who raped my sister because they are still living. Because this book is now in the hands of many people who know me, I am sure that eventually these men will read this book and realize that I know the truth about what happened. I do not want this book to be a stumbling block in their lives; I do not want the information in these pages to prevent them from knowing Christ our Savior. Instead, I want it to be a blessing because of the power of forgiveness. I pray that God touches their hearts and gives them conviction of their sins so that they may repent. Earlier, I stated that my mother's desire to end my life was not her doing but a plan of the enemy; likewise, what happened to my sister was not a design of men but of the enemy who wanted to destroy her life.

"[12]For we do not wrestle against flesh and blood, but against principalities, against powers, against the rulers of the darkness of this age, against spiritual hosts of wickedness in the heavenly places."
Ephesians 6.12

My mother's behavior never ceased to amaze me. She was certainly unpredictable. For instance, sometimes she would behave like a lioness, defending us against the wickedness of the world, and other times she behaved totally different; as if there was something inside of her (almost diabolical) that dominated her behavior. To give you an idea of what I am saying, I will share a moment that caused me to see my mother in a totally different way. I recall the day that my brother dropped the eggs he was carrying. My mother's reaction was shocking; neither my brother nor I expected what happened next. She punished him severely, but it was not enough as far as she was concerned. As if controlled by some unseen force, she grabbed my brother's small frame and dragged him to a nearby tree where she hanged him. Again, I felt frozen in time as I watched one more unexplained event unfold before my eyes. One thought raced through my mind: She is going to kill him. There was no doubt in my mind that my brother would not survive the punishment for his crime. My fears increased when mom told me that I had to keep watch that night in another house that was under our care. Though I desperately wanted to stay, I knew I could not disobey mom.

As I walked away from what was happening to my brother, a feeling of impotence swept all over me. I spent that night in a house alone with thoughts and images that invaded my dreams. The next day, having obeyed my mother's orders, I ran home as fast as my little legs could carry me. I needed to know what had happened to my brother. I desperately looked for him when I arrived home, and I found him. He was covered in blood from the countless bruises inflicted by my mother's rage — his neck colorfully displaying the mark of the rope that held his small body. I cannot tell you how many images and mixed emotions I experienced at that moment. How could a mother do such a thing to her child? How could a mother who is willing to give up her life to protect her child want to destroy him?

Like I said before, my mother's behavior never ceased to amaze me. She could be the most level-headed woman one moment, and a crazed person the next. Her roller coaster emotions affected my own. Though I was young, the things that I had experienced up until that day had somehow damaged me. I would look at my mother and all I could feel was contempt, bitterness, and fear.

Please do not misunderstand me. At the time, I was young and naive. I did not see the truth of what was really happening with my mother. Now that I am a grown woman, a mother, and a wife, I have learned to see things from a different perspective. As children, we perceive things one way, but when we grow up the scenery changes. Paul said:

> *"[11] When I was a child, I spoke as a child, I understood as a child, I thought as a child; but when I became a man, I put away childish things."*
> *I Corinthians 13.11*

The ministry of deliverance is a mystery that I understand. That is why I know that the devil tries to destroy families by using individuals. I have said this twice, and now I will say it again: it was not my mother — it was all a part of the devil's master plan to destroy each member of my family. By the time you finish reading this book, you will understand why he was so determined to destroy us and why it is important for me that you understand this truth.

When last I mentioned how I felt about my mother, I said that I felt contempt, bitterness, and fear, yet I never judged her actions; I simply did not understand them. When I look back at her life, I become painfully aware of the hardship that she had to endure; her life was not pleasant. May the Lord guard my heart from ever passing judgment against her.

As difficult as my mother was, she was different towards me. She treated me differently than the rest of her children. She used to say to me, "Chelito, someday I am going to take you out of this place so that you don't have to suffer what I have gone through." She was not lying. At the age of 11, I left the small country town of La Joya to live with my aunt in the big city of Bogota. It hurt to leave my home and my family, but leaving my younger sister in the situation that she was in made me feel worse. I was heart-broken to know that mom had no plans to take her out of that place of torture and pain. I felt like a knife had pierced my heart as I walked away. The day I left La Joya I was a woman trapped in a little girl's body — the Lord revealed it to me one day in a dream.

In only a short time, you already know a lot about my childhood and some of my early memories which are full of traumatic experiences, sadness, loneliness, frustrations, and resentment; yet, God's hand was always on my life protecting me in very special ways.

The City of Bogota and my Teenage Years

Life in the city was not what I expected. If the thought ever entered my mind that life was going to get easier, I was wrong. The dreams of a child quickly vanished, and in its place, the nightmare of growing up alone became a reality.

Bogota and La Joya were complete opposites in every sense of the word. Yet one thing was still the same: I had to work very hard to earn my daily meal. My aunt and I arrived in Bogota where I would live with her for the next 3 years. Once settled in her house, I was directed to my "new profession". She forced me to work very hard at her drinking establishment called "La Estrada" which catered to the neighborhood drunks. Among the many responsibilities that required my attention, I was also responsible for selling beer — which was hauled in a cart — around the neighborhood. The reward for my labor was the privilege of sleeping on the hard floor of her house until my 14th birthday.

I should mention that although she used me for personal gain and never gave me monetary compensation for the work that I did for her, she did take care of me — in her own way. She protected me from the perverts that visited her bar; she kept me safe from physical harm; and she made sure that no one had an opportunity to corrupt me — basically, she kept me from going down the wrong path. She tried very hard to keep my naive lifestyle and innocence intact. During the three years that I lived with my aunt, I never drunk beer, smoked cigarettes, or used drugs.

Life was hard in Bogota. On certain days, half the morning would pass without a bite of food to touch my lips. To make matters worse, I kept burning the pots whenever I tried to cook something for myself on the days that we had food. Please keep in mind that I knew how to cook over on open fire for many people, not on gas stoves for a party of one. I had no idea how to use the gas stove. Since I was hungry and without money, my only option was to steal a couple of pesos from my aunt to buy an empanada which is a beef patty. Solving the problem of hunger was nothing compared to the time when a couple of men tried to rape me; this happened on two separate occasions. To this day, I believe these men failed at their attempt to harm me because I had learned how to take care of myself by watching my mother; plus, I had the determination and the strength to defend myself. Praise God for His supernatural protection!

Three years passed and life did not seem to get any better. I needed a change, but change implied having knowledge which I did not have. Do you remember when I told you about my school experience? To finish that story, I should say that I never really had the chance to learn; I never finished elementary school — not even first grade. Realizing that I was completely illiterate made me feel hate towards my parents for not doing what was necesary to ensure my education. At that moment, I made a crucial decision that changed my life forever. I decided to leave my aunt's house — sleeping on the floor and working for free. On my road to learning, I found a place to live and my first job "with pay" at a restaurant called Los Olivos; it was owned and operated by people who were known as "evangelicals". The couple that owned this restaurant took very good care of me. As my aunt had done before them, they did what was necesary to protect my innocence and keep me safe from danger. Though they were Christians, I did not receive the Lord as my personal Savior while I lived with them because they had a terrible testimony — most of the time. They knew how to preach the gospel, but they did not practice what they preached. I was one of several people that worked at Los Olivos Restaurant and who paid this couple for room and board. Besides the fact that we were paid a measly salary for our hard work, this couple would deduct from each worker's paycheck enough money to cover the expenses of room and board, which included water, light, and oil; after their deductions, there was hardly any money left for us.

Little by little, the shade of innocence that embraced my life started to fade. This "awakening" led me to make one of many life changing decisions. I decided to search for a teacher who could help compensate, as if by some miraculous way, the years of schooling that I had lost. I found such a person who tested my level of knowledge in the basics of reading, writing, and mathematical skills. The results of these tests traumatized me because it confirmed that I was illiterate. Once I managed to accept this truth, I went back to the teacher who told me that I had to start from the beginning. At age 16, I completed first grade. A month later, I graduated from second grade. Six months later,

I was promoted to the third grade, and so on. Every six months, I was promoted to the next level. What an incredible and difficult experience that was! Remember, I was 16 years old at the time, living in Bogota, on my own, and working full time. Learning the basics at the age of 16 was a challenge that I met with great opposition. I was often humiliated and told by people that I was a dumb brute; they mortified me by saying that I would never amount to anything in life — they were wrong. Today, I lack the words to express my appreciation for the help that I received at that school. Who would have thought the day I found out I was illiterate would become the first step to my writing this book?

And the learning process continued. This time it had nothing to do with reading or writing; it had to do with the normal process of development for a young woman. I had my first menstrual cycle. Since no one had ever mentioned that this would be coming, I was troubled when it did; I had no idea why I was bleeding or what was happening to me. I started to wonder what other experiences awaited me. What else was out there that I was not aware of? I would soon find out.

Two years later, at the age of 18 and after seven years since I had left with my aunt to Bogota, I returned home. My brothers and sisters looked at me and wondered who I was; they were confused. Seven years can change a person; I left a child and returned a woman. I looked at them and said, "Don't you recognize me? I am Chelito, your sister. I left when I was 11 years old." Once I said these words, they realized I was their sister. They were very happy to see me, but they did not know if to cry or to laugh, for standing before them was a woman, not a child, totally different than the person they remembered. I visited with my family for only four days; I could not stay any longer. I was not prepared for what I experienced next. When I saw my parents, a storm of emotions swept through me like a hurricane. My rejection towards my parents had grown deep. So deep in fact, that I could not stand to be there one more day. I returned to the city, but this time, I did not leave alone. My sister Lucia begged me to take her with me. She desperately cried out saying, "Help me; help me; take me away from this place." I knew the reason for her desperate desire to leave La Joya, and I did not hesitate in my response. On our way to Bogota, she recounted everything that she had experienced during my absence; she confessed that the sexual abuse that I had witnessed many years ago had not stopped. As she shared her experiences, bitterness and resentment made their ugly way into every fiber of my existence.

Choosing Between God and the Devil...

After Lucia and I settled in Bogota, I met a man and fell in love with him; he was a dream come true. This man, who shall remain nameless, invited me to live with him, but this was not the proposal that I was hoping for. My response to his invitation was: "If you think that living with you in sin is what I want, then you are sadly mistaken." I have always had strong convictions as to what I wanted, and although I was firm in my decision, I still suffered greatly because I loved this man. Yet, he was very persistent and did not give up. He continued to call me until I agreed to go out with him again. We dated for a while during which time we got to know each other a little better. He continued to pursue the idea of us living together, but I was more determined than ever to stand my ground and continued to say no. I took very good care of myself while I was with him, and I controlled my desires because I did not want to fail in my convictions. I wanted to remain pure until marriage. I knew that I wanted to wait and experience intimacy with a man after the marriage vows were said.

I remember that when I was 11 years old, unaware that I was making a covenant with God, I said, "God, I want you to be with me 24 hours a day, and I want you to help me meet a man that will be with me for a lifetime." Funny how things work out; I looked to a God that I barely knew to give me comfort and strength during difficult times. I suppose I always felt a special passion for God, and although I did not know it at the time, it was the same passion that my father had for God. Setting aside the fact that neither my father nor I knew who God really was, something inside of us assured us that He was real; that He existed. I know my father loved God because he taught us that we had to fear Him. I remember that my father would remove his hat and say, "The day I leave this earth I will be with God because my faith will take me to heaven." I know that his knowledge about God was very limited; it was small town faith. Nevertheless, my father believed that God existed and he taught his children to fear God and to beleive in Him. Praise God for the day that we learned the whole truth!

Getting back to the "love of my life," I thought he would be the only one for me. However, during a civic strike in Colombia, on June 10, 1985, Jesus came into my life and replaced him. My new found love in Jesus did not deter this man from insisting that we should live together and "experience" life. My answer this time was: "Our relationship must end because I just met Jesus, and because of Him, you will leave my life forever." My decision to end my relationship with this man almost destroyed me; I cried for two months. To get me through the sadness of his absence, I asked the Lord to tear him from my heart and end the love that I felt for him; He did. This was not an easy request for me to ask God because beyond looking for love in a man, I was really looking for a father figure to protect me. When my relationship with this man ended, I came to the realization that I had grown very dependent on him. I was also able to visualize, through God's gift of discernment, what my life with this man would be like had I stayed with him. I saw my future in a dream; I dreamed that he was a shameless drunk and that the only thing on his mind was to lead me down the road to destruction.

Who we are today is the result of the good and bad decisions that we make, but sometimes, we want to blame God or others for our circumstances. We must understand that when we make bad choices we will reap bad results. In my case, I had to decide between Jesus and the devil. I felt that God said to me, "I place before you two choices, do you want blessings or ruin?" Of course, I chose the path of blessing, but I must admit that the most "appealing" to my flesh was the one to destruction.

Today, I understand that the devil had this man under his control because he would say terrible things about pastors and Christians. For instance, he said that pastors abused young women like me. Each time I heard him say things like these, I ignored him. I am thankful that chapter of my life is over. Praise God for Jesus. His loving protection kept me from making a big mistake and made it possible for me to meet Guillermo Maldonado — my husband. Had I not chosen Jesus of Nazareth who knows where I would be right now!

The Most Important Day of my Life...

I already shared with you that during my relationship with the "nameless" gentleman, I met Jesus - Lord and Savior of my life, but now I want to tell you how that wonderful day, the day I accepted Jesus into my life, came about.

I should start by giving you a little bit of background about the person responsible for the blessing of my salvation. I do not know all of the details about her life, but what I know, you will also know.

In Bogota, there was a wealthy Colombian woman who held a high position in government; her profession kept her very busy and always surrounded by people. However, on one of those appointment filled days, someone approached her and shared with her the good news of the gospel, the saving grace and power of Jesus Christ. I really do not know what her life was like before Jesus, but her answer to His invitation of salvation changed the path of her life and mine forever!

Soon after she received Jesus in her heart, she decided to resign from her position in government; she put away her suits, high heels, briefcase, and walked away from a profession that provided a high standard of living. Instead, she put on a pair of jeans and sneakers, and with her Bible under her arm, she started to preach the gospel on the streets of Bogota. She went door to door telling anyone who was willing to listen to the good news of God's redeeming grace; she also shared the testimony of what God had done for her and how He had transformed her life.

On June 10, 1985, after knocking on many doors, she came to mine. She knocked on the door, and I answered it. What an amazing thing to realize that the simple act of answering a knock on the door can transform a life forever! Did you know that Jesus is always knocking at the door of our hearts? Are we answering His call and welcoming Him in?

> *"20Behold, I stand at the door and knock. If anyone hears My voice and opens the door, I will come in to him and dine with him, and he with Me."*
> Revelation 3.20

Her name was Luisa — the beautiful woman of God who dared to knock at my door not knowing what would happen when it was opened — I sincerely hope that someday she realizes the impact that a simple knock on the door did for me and how God used her as an instrument of blessing that transformed my life forever. After telling me about Jesus and the fact that He loves me so much that He surrendered His life at the cross for me, she explained that I was a sinner and that my sin separated me from Him. She also said that if I believed that Jesus was the Son of God and that He gave His life for me at the cross, I would be saved. Before the invitation to accept Jesus, she went ahead and shared her personal testimony of salvation; thus, the reason why I have a few details about her life. After she was done, I remember she asked me what I consider to be the most important question that any of us could be asked: "Would you like to receive Jesus into your heart today?" You know what my answer was: "Yes!" One three-letter word changed the direction of my life — from eternal separation from God to eternal life with God. After the hugs, kisses, and suggestions as to what I was supposed to do now that I was a born-again Christian, Luisa invited me to attend her church.

When we arrived, she introduced me to an 85 year old man; he was a handsome senior citizen with white hair and a gentle voice. After the proper introductions were made, she asked him to pray for me. I remember her words clearly: "I want you to pray for this girl." He accepted her request and prayed for me; he placed his hand on my head as he lifted my life to Jesus. I am not entirely clear on all the words he said at that moment, but I do remember the sweet special warmth that seemed to penetrate every fiber of my being. I felt like a brilliant light pierced my heart and mind at that instant. Although I was new to the Christian experience, I was certain that at that moment the Spirit of God entered my life in a very special way; it was a sweet, Spirit filled moment in which I felt God's loving arms embrace me and protect me. He was exactly what I had been yearning for my entire life. That moment was the first of many wonderful and beautiful experiences that I have had in my journey with God, and as beautiful as these experiences have been, that day in that little church, under the touch of a loving gray-haired man, I experienced the love of God like never before. At that moment, I knew that I would follow Jesus forever!

My Sister Lucia...

My new found life in Jesus made me want to share it with everyone I knew. The first person on my list was my sister Lucia. I would invite her to attend church with me but she was not very interested in what the pastor had to say; she fell asleep during every service that I managed to get her to attend. My sister would say to me, "I just don't want to go to church; I don't like evangelicals." Had I known then what I know now about deliverance and how to set the captives free, I might have been able to help her. However, since I did not know anything about deliverance or how the devil can hold us captive, I did the next best thing and invited her to church.

I never saw Lucia give her life to Christ. Her mind always seemed to be on other things and other places. One day, she confessed her desire to move away; she wanted to leave the city and start a new life. I heard what she had to say but did not agree with her decision. I was very bold and firm with her; I told her that she should stay because the place where she was going was very dangerous. Nevertheless, my warnings went unheard; she packed her belongings and left; she went from bad to worse in a very short time. Lucia met a man and in the midst of her chaotic life, she became pregnant. Towards the end of her pregnancy, an extremely poisionous snake bit her. She was quickly rushed to the hospital where the doctors informed her that the venum had travelled very quickly through her blood stream causing the baby's blood to be seriously contaminated. According to the doctors, the baby only had 11 grams of uncontaminated blood in her system. The doctors worked tiredlessly to save Lucia and her baby, and although they were successful in their efforts to save their lives, not all was as it should be. The snake's venum caused the baby to develop a rare skin condition that spotted her skin. These were the words that were told to me to describe the baby's appearance: "Her skin looked like the skin of a snake." How far away from the truth that is, I do not know. In any case, Lucia and her baby were saved that day. The baby grew up — spots and all — but she was never quite the same as the other children. The damage caused by the snake's venom went deeper than her skin; it caused severe learning disabilities. Two years after that fateful day, my sister suffered yet another tragic moment in her life; her baby girl died.

Lucia was not the same after her daughter's death. To add to her pain and growing depression, her husband continued to abuse her in every way imaginable. Unable to cope with the terrible circumstances of her life, Lucia committed suicide; at least this is the official statement of her death. To this day, it is still unclear what really happened; I was not there when she died, nor was I aware that Lucia was suffering so much, and although people say that she committed suicide, in my heart I feel that she did not die by her own hand; I believe that she was murdered. After I was informed of her death, I inquired about her life. Many said to me that Lucia would constantly say: "Chelito will get me through this." I wish I had known what she was going through; I would have done everything within my power to save her from her tragic destiny.

I have asked the Lord many times to tell me where she is; in heaven or..., but He has not answered. I hope, with all my heart, that before she took her last breath, she remembered the knock at the door of her heart and invited Jesus to come into her life; I pray that the saving power of Jesus Christ and His unending love embraced her during those last moments of life. I know that I cannot do anything more for Lucia, but I can do something for you. Too often, we wait to make the most important decision of our lives for later; tomorrow mom; tomorrow Chelito; tomorrow Jesus. Do not wait like Lucia waited. Do not fall asleep while Jesus knocks at your door. Change the course of your life today!

The day I met Jesus, I cried a lot and thanked Him for His super-natural protection over my life. I realize now that the direction of my life could have resembled Lucia's had I not accepted Jesus. Sadly, she died at the young age of 26. Her entire life was full of cruelty and pain — most of which can never be told. When I think about Lucia and her childhood, I remember that my moth-er seemed to always be displeased or annoyed with her. I never understood why mom disliked her so much; I think it must have been something spiritual, for there is no other way to describe her strange attitude towards Lucia. My mother would speak very harsh and cruel words at this little girl. She was nasty and direct about her feelings towards her. Without knowing it, mother placed Lucia in danger with the confessions of her mouth. The words of our mouths have power; there is power in our tongue. A warning to all parents: be very careful with what you say to your children and grandchildren.

> "*"A wholesome **tongue** is a tree of life, but perverseness in it breaks the spirit." Proverbs 15.4*

> *"[21]Death and life are in the power of the **tongue**." Proverbs 18.21*

Good Bye to Hate, Frustration, and Bitterness...

> *"[2]Honor your father and mother," which is the first commandment with promise: [3]that it may be well*

with you and you may live long on the earth."
Ephesians 6.2, 3

I was 21 years old when I surrendered my life to the Lord. Once I made that decision, I knew there was no turning back. A deep hunger to read His Word and to know Him exploded inside of me. The more I read His Word, the more I trusted in Him. My relationship with Jesus was strengthened and His Word began to erase, little by little, the hate, bitterness, resentment, and anger that were rooted in me. One verse that the Lord continually placed in my heart was: Ephesians 6.2; this was one of many revelations that confronted me.

"²Honor your father and mother," which is the first commandment with promise."

I lost track of how many times I have read this verse. When I finally understood the meaning of it, I knew that I had to forgive my parents for every terrible thing that I suffered through, including that of my siblings. It is easy to forgive a lie, or one moment of betrayal, but a lifetime of pain and injustice was going to take a little longer — or so I thought. When our heart's desire is to honor God, we will have the strength to do what is necesary to obey His Word; I forgave my parents, but this was only the beginning of the wonderful adventure that I am now in. Forgiving is the first step to the healing process of our heart. When we forgive our parents, or those who hurt us, we must also learn to honor them — with our time, words of affirmation, and with our monetary gifts; we must respect and speak well of them.

When the full revelation of "honor thy father and mother" entered my spirit, my first act of obedience was to return to my hometown; the place where my parents lived. I needed to ask their forgiveness for judging and blaming them for every painful event in my life. I pray that you understand what I am about to say, but up until that day, I had not understood that they, too, had suffered greatly and were deeply hurt; I was not the only victim in the game of life. When we understand that we are not the only victims, and that people often behave in ways that reflect their own pain, then the forgiveness process can begin. I was not expecting what came next. My expression of forgiveness was rejected; many factors could have affected their reaction but the one that I believe was the strongest was their strong "religious" background; my mother was an idolater; she worshipped idols made of bronze and wood. When they heard my pleading for forgiveness, they criticized my behavior and branded me a fanatic and crazy evangelical. My reaction was equally as strong; I made an inward decision at that time: "If you think I am a fanatic now, wait and see what I will become; this is an experience that cannot be explained."

Still new to the gospel, and unaware of the existence of the deliverance ministry, my only choice was to finish what I had started — which was to ask forgiveness — and left La Joya yet again. To the naked eye one might think that nothing happened that day I visited my family and asked their forgiveness, but in time, I understood that our first deliverance takes place the moment that we accept Jesus; that moment of repentance when we recognize that we are sinners and ask Jesus to forgive us becomes the first step in our deliverance from bondage; the second step to deliverance is forgiveness. Every time we forgive and ask forgiveness, we grow as Christians and mature in Christ.

Since that wonderful day, June 10th, 1985, I have matured and increased my understanding in spiritual matters. Little by little, God has chipped away at the layers of pain that surrounded my heart; He has held my hand every step of the way; guiding me gently through the process of deliverance from the bitterness, hate, resentment, and the many traumatic events that I endured throughout my childhood. The Lord set me free from the anger that I felt because of the things that I had witnessed and suffered; He rescued me from the prison of pain that kept me captive to the memory of my mother's suffering.

To protect our frail hearts, it is the tendency of most human beings to create shelters or to build walls between us and that which causes us pain. Sometimes, we do not realize that the anger and pain that we desperately try to escape from is already stored in our subconscious. Because of this stored anger in my spirit, the Lord had to confront me. It has always been my heart's desire to help women recover from the pain of their past and to help them look forward to a new and bright future in Christ. However, although I was passionate about this calling in my life, there was something still inside of me that was not right — it was something that kept me from identifing myself with other women. That something was anger; it was holding me captive in my mother's world of resentment for being a woman.

Do you remember when I told you that my mother wished she had been born a man and that according to her, men did not suffer as much as women? She hated being a woman; it was a curse to her. To her, being a woman was equal to suffering and pain. I do not remember seeing mom smile; she was always sad and on the verge of tears. Her attitude towards women stayed with me; it was buried deep within my subconscious, and it was affecting me and my relationship with other women. Praise God for the ministry of deliverance and the power of forgiveness. Today, I am no longer captive to those memories or pain. God can take a broken heart and make it whole again. His perfect love restores and delivers us!

Years later, my mother heard the message of salvation and received Jesus as her personal Savior; soon after, she left to be with the Lord. My father also received Jesus during a time when he was hospitalized and at the point of death. When I heard of his condition, I went to be with him during those critical moments. I remember sitting by his hospital bed watching him take each breath with great effort; he looked tired. I started to gently caress his head while telling him what a wonderful father he had been; I thanked him for teaching me good moral values and for the practical teachings that I had received from him. The love of God that was pouring out of me strengthened his body and healed his soul that day. Not only was he miraculously healed, he was also saved — Jesus entered his life that day. Today, he is a blossoming Christian and the cofounder of the church that we have in Colombia. He is a warrior in God's army and a man that practices fasting and prayer. My parents and most of my brothers and sisters are strong Christians today. And because of the power of love and forgiveness, many of my mother's dreams for them are now becoming a reality. We are the perfect example of how God can save one life and transform nations. The glory belongs to Him!

I witnessed how the enemy tried to destroy my family, but his plans against us failed because God has His own plans for us. We are covered by His covenant of redemption. My brothers and sisters are powerful men and women of prayer — transformed, free, and restored thanks to the unconditional love of our Lord Jesus Christ.

The First Prayer that was Miraculously Answered...

Let us return once more to Bogota where I was still struggling to make each day a good day. I was 22 and working at a leather factory where I worked for a man who constantly sexually harrassed me. One day, during the course of a regular workday, my boss called me into his office and asked me to bring him a mint candy. On my way to complying with his request, I was distracted with other things and completely forgot to get his candy. Moments later, I was ushered into his office where he completely humiliated me (I guess he really loved mint candy). He offended and insulted me until finally he spoke the dreaded words that no one wants to hear from their employers: "You are fired! You will never amount to anything. You are nobody and I don't understand why you waste your time trying to learn anything." The words of rejection and abuse rolled off his tongue with ease; the words of his mouth revealed the contempt that he felt towards me because I never accepted his sexual advances or innuendos. His words filled me with such anger that I responded with: "Someday, God will declare how He is going to deal with you." Once I said this, I fell to my knees feeling totally humiliated. I cried out to God saying: "Get me out of this place. I want to learn and I can't. I want to meet a nice man, but the only thing that men want is to use women as if they were objects or as if we were disposable trash. Get me out of this place and out of this cursed poverty."

I left that man's office in tears, but a month after that humiliating experience and after losing my job, he called me back into his office. I thought about it once or twice before returning to that place, but finally the curiousity had the best of me; I had to find out what he wanted. After the respectful greetings were over, he said: "I summoned you because the owner of the company needs to speak with you. He asked me if I knew of an honest young woman, and I said yes. I briefly described you to him and he "still" wants to meet you." His instructions were for me to go to the owner's mansion — which took over an entire block in his neighborhood called "El Chico", in Bogota. On arrival, I was met by a Jewish-American woman who instantly said to me, "I have interviewed twenty women, but you are the one that I need. Will you stay with me? I travel a lot, and I need a person to accompany me on all my travels. We will be traveling to the United States; therefore, I need you to go to the United States Embassy and solicit a visa. Begin to ask for God's favor so that the United States Counselor can stamp your passport and grant your visa." Before going to the US Embassy, I asked God, "Lord, please grant me grace and favor; help me so that my visa application is not denied." When I arrived at the embassy, the person responsible for the approval or denial of visa applications simply looked at me from behind the customer's window and asked me something that I do not remember today, but his words are not important because he approved my application for a visa and handed it to me.

My new boss and I traveled to the United States but did not stay very long; soon, we were back in Colombia. Many Christians worked for this lady and her husband; one day, one of my co-workers had a dream. He described his dream to the staff and together we came to the conclusion that danger was near and that something was about to happen in that house. His suggestion was for us to pray. As predicted, a short time later, a band of kidnappers forced their way through the company's guards with plans of kidnapping the owner of the company. Their attempt to kidnap the owner failed because they took an employee who looked just like the owner. What came next was of no surprise to anyone; the owner of the company immediately took his family and traveled to the United States leaving me behind in Colombia. Before leaving, his wife said to me, "Honey, you cannot come with me right now." She and her family left to the United States but not before leaving instructions for me to follow and meet them there later on.

The answer to my prayer had just been handed to me. I considered it a miracle that one day, in the office of a man who hurt me, I would ask God to take me from that wretched place and a short time later that prayer was answered. With my American visa in one hand, and the Bible in the other, I got on the plane that would take me to the American Dream; I could not help but to wonder what surprises God had in store for me.

CHAPTER II

THE AMERICAN DREAM

From a Remote Town in Colombia to the American Dream, the United States...

My legs trembled as I stepped into that airplane. I was very nervous about flying and about the new life that waited for me. The United States had only been part of a map in my geography book up until that day, and now I was going to live there, alone. I was so tense that I sat in the wrong seat — the flight attendant had to take me to the right one: Seat No. 20. Not knowing what to do, I sat down where I was told and started to do what was familiar to me; I read the Bible. I could trust and depend on the words found in that wonderful book; I knew that if all else failed, His Word would not fail. The woman who sat next to me was very beautiful; she noticed that I was reading the Bible and asked me, "Are you a Christian?" My answer to her was, "I'm trying to be." During the flight, she went ahead and shared a little bit about herself; she told me that she was a missionary working in Miami. To me, she was like an angel sent from heaven who kept me from falling apart on the airplane and who helped me at the airport through the process of immigration. But she did not stop there; she also drove me to the house where the Jewish family was waiting for me and left me with her blessing.

The family welcomed me as if they were seeing an old friend. I worked two years for this Jewish family where I was able to model the testimony of Jesus through my behavior. I loved God and wanted to honor Him; I also started to dig deeper into His Word and to seek God wholeheartedly. My relationship and love for God was obvious, and this family knew it well. One day, the lady of the house fainted; when I saw her on the floor, my first instinct was to pray for her — this proved to be the right thing to do because in less than three minutes she was off the floor and ready to continue with her daily agenda. Every time any member of this family had a problem they could not resolve, they would call on me to pray and seek God's favor on their behalf. According to them, I was closer to God because my prayers were heard and answered.

For the next two years, life was uneventful until my visa expired. For anyone who understands what it is like to be an illegal immigrant in this country, you should know that it was not the best situation to be in. Wealthy men pursued me; they proposed marriage and offered to legalize my legal status, but praise God that I never accepted any of their proposals. I said to Jesus, "Lord, you brought me into this country, and I trust that You will legalize my status and somehow approve my residency. I will not lie, and I will do everything the way you want me to do it." Now that I think about it, everytime that God was about to do something life-changing in my life, the enemy would jump right in and try to disuade me from His plans; Praise God that the Lord had already established His plans for my life, and I was confident that He was going to finish what He started in me.

> *"13...till we all come to the unity of the faith and of the knowledge of the Son of God, to a perfect man, to the measure of the stature of the fullness of Christ; 14that we should no longer be children, tossed to and fro and carried about with every wind of doctrine, by the trickery of men, in the cunning craftiness of deceitful plotting."*
> *Ephesians 4.13-14*

My Husband: Guillermo Maldonado

Life in the United States was different, but the commitment that I had made to Jesus the day that I was born-again was still the same. My desire to know God on a deeper level increased as I heard and studied His Word. One thing that I was certain about was that I needed to attend a church to continue in my journey with God; and so I did. I started to attend a wonderful church where I experienced wonderful times with Jesus. It was not easy for me to attend church because I was alone; I had to persevere in my quest for that relationship with God without anyone to encourage me or to keep me company. However, it was in that church where I met Guillermo — I did not know it at the time, but he was to be my future husband. Guillermo was a baby Christian; he had invited Jesus into his life only five months before we met. He was a young man who was beginning to learn how to be in this world but not of this world; as a matter of fact, he was still dealing with certain worldly behavior that made me uneasy; he loved to flirt — for weeks I noticed that he would not take his eyes of me. One Sunday, after weeks of watching me, he decided to make his move and approached me. One of the many things that I love and admire about Guillermo is his ability to persevere; I say this because the first time that he came within reach of me my immediate response was to rebuke the devil — I am sure that the expression on my face reflected my thoughts. I kept saying inside of me: "Devil, I am not in church to look for a husband." I lost track of how many times I rebuked him in my mind, but regardless of how I felt, he never gave up on me — we became best friends.

After that first encounter, we saw each other once a week and spoke on the phone up to three times a day. Regardless of how many times we spoke on the phone or saw each other, our growing friendship did not stop me from thinking that his inter-est in me was purely a selfish one; my expectation of that rela-tionship never went beyond believing that he was going to make me fall in love with him only to leave me when he felt that there was nothing more that he could get from me. I was almost 23 years old and I was sure that the only reason he wanted to be near me was because he wanted to play with my emotions. To my surprise, every thought about him that I had allowed to swim around in my mind stopped the moment that he asked me to be his girlfriend.

Guillermo and I had grown to love the Lord and each other's company, but we also knew that if we were to take our friendship into the next level, we needed to take a step back and seek God's guidance for our lives. We wanted to honor God and do His will — our decision to have a more serious relationship rested on what the Lord would speak to our spirits. For that reason, we both agreed to fast and pray for the next three months. At the end of this time, we would make our final decision concerning his proposal to take our friendship into the next level. We also agreed that if our relationship was not God's will, we would go our separate ways. We had an incredible friendship and were careful not to allow anything into our lives that could damage it; there was a strong spiritual bond between the two of us.

I find this a little difficult to admit right now because even though we were considering taking our relationship into a more serious level, we still seemed to dislike each other at other levels; we rarely agreed on anything — he was choleric and short-tempered, and I was extremely melancholic. I agreed to the three months of fasting in prayer because in my mind, I assumed that our "let's wait and see" time would be long enough to prove that he was not serious about our relationship or me. Nevertheless, regardless of my insecurities, those three months were wonderful because it was a time when our friendship grew in a very special way. We started to build a spiritual dependency with each other; it was not a carnal dependency but a spiritual one. After this time of fasting and prayer, we both felt that it was God's will for us to be together and so Guillermo and I became engaged.

During our courtship, I lived an hour away from Miami. The people that I lived with were Edy and Juanita, a Puerto Rican family who loved me as if I was their own daughter. If they ever read this book, I want them to know that I appreciate everything that they did for me; I consider them to be very special people in my life.

Although I had been living in the United States for a while and was engaged to Guillermo, somewhere in the back of my mind I thought that I was only here temporarily. At the time, I was employed cleaning office buildings and houses, yet my plans for the future included working hard to save enough money to return to Colombia and finish school — I wanted to fulfill my dream of having my own boutique where high fashion designs would be created for the well-to-do clientele, but God had other plans. While engaged to Guillermo, my love for God increased. Everywhere I went, I told people about Jesus — in the street, in the bus, and everywhere.

After two years of engagement, Guillermo and I made an appointment to speak to our pastor because we wanted to know what he thought of our relationship. After hearing what we had to say, his response blessed us because he said that he saw something great in our lives as a result of our union. We walked out of his office more certain than ever that we were meant to be together. After that day, we waited yet another two years through which we had to overcome strong obstacles.

After years of waiting on God, the prayer that I had made long ago, at the age of 11, was finally answered on October 8, 1988. Guillermo and I got married. You might find this hard to believe but my wedding was the first that I had ever attended. Our Pastors Jesus and Cony Del Cristo were wonderful people who treated us with love and respect, especially the day of our wedding. Since I had never attended a wedding, I had no idea what this event entailed; they helped us organize it and made sure that every detail was taken care of, including ordering the flowers. I had a beautiful wedding; the color scheme was white and blue, as the Lord commands! That wonderful day in October was the beginning of our marriage, and also, I believe it was the birth of our ministry.

The beginning of our marriage and ministry was rough. One of the greatest trials that we had to overcome was our own marital relationship. Guillermo and I brought into our new relationship as husband and wife the pain from our childhoods and the feelings of rejection that were deeply rooted in our spirits. Without realizing what was happening, these feelings caused me to reject him and vice versa. If you recall, I said that I had experienced rejection from the moment of conception; this feeling of rejection had seeped into the very marrow of my existence. Demons of rejection and unforgiveness, that could or ever would exist, were operating in me. As if this were not enough for one person to deal with, there was also a spirit of shame that had been drilled into me by my mother for the mere fact that I was a woman.

I know first hand what it means to be in bondage by tormenting spirits and that is why no one can dissuade me from the truth on deliverance. I am a living testimony of someone who was in desperate need of deliverance. Guillermo was also suffering the effects of rejection because he grew up without a mother since the tender age of four; he was raised by his stepmother who was not the kindest person towards him. Can you imagine what it means to a small child to grow up without a mother? The spirits of abandonment and rejection that were operating in him were clearly evident. Nonetheless, he was fortunate enough to have the ability and the opportunity to learn. His father made every effort to ensure that he would attend school and complete his studies.

As I look into our past and compare our upbringing, I realize that although we grew up in different geographical locations, surrounded by different types of people and things, the outcome of our lives was very similar; we grew up in much the same type of atmosphere — feeling abandoned and rejected by the people that should have been there to protect us. As I travel through the early years of our marriage, I am keenly aware that the bond that kept us together, the one thing that kept our marriage alive, was not the love that we had for each other but the fear of the Lord; this fear was the thermometer that kept us in check with each other and in our ministry every day.

On our wedding day, we also made the commitment to pray together every day, as a couple. I strongly believe that our commitment to prayer is an important pillar that has contributed to the success of our marriage. For a long time, the circumstances surrounding our lives were not in our favor; we did not have any guarantees that our relationship would last, but our decision to base our marriage on the love and fear of the Lord gave it stability.

Bryan, my First Son

Soon after we were married, Guillermo and I received the wonderful news that we were expecting our first child. In addition to our joy of becoming parents, Guillermo was also blessed with his first missionary trip to Honduras which came about when I was eight months pregnant. I remember crying out to God saying: "Lord, I do not understand how you can send Guillermo away on a missionary trip when I am so close to the end of my pregnancy." Our financial situation was not optimal at the time; there was no money for food or rent during this pregnancy. My countless prayers were soon answered through a man of God who said that I should not worry because the Lord was going to supply for our every need. This man also said that God was going to prosper us financially and that the time was coming when I would not have to worry about any of these things again — God was going to provide. These words were refreshing and wonderful to hear, but the provision that we were hoping for did not come immediately; the Lord tested our faith in such matters as trusting Him for our financial needs.

Bryan, our first son, came during a very difficult time in our marriage. I remember the days when there was barely enough money to buy pampers or baby food. We were in a serious financial predicament because although Guillermo was working, his income was not enough for a family of three. As for me, I had no problem finding jobs, but when the employers found out that I did not have the proper documentation such as a social security number or work permits, they would fire me. You see, I had made up my mind long ago that I was going to be honest about my residency status; I was not going to lie because I believed that God would always provide. I wanted to honor and obey Him. Losing a job never discouraged me from doing what I had to do; I had learned to work hard, and I knew that God would make a way; after all, He is our Jehovah Jireh.

I decided, if I could not work for a company, I was going to become an entrepeneur, and so, I started to sell home-cooked meals; I also offered child care services from my home because I did not want to leave my baby with strangers. I worked hard and made every effort to help my husband with the financial responsibility of our home because I did not want him to carry the burden alone. Also, I was determined not to give up or to become a welfare recipient. I had learned early on that to survive in life, one has to work very hard — Praise God that my parents taught me to be a hard-working woman!

With Bryan now occupying a major part of my day, and Guillermo traveling so much as an evangelist, our relationship as a couple was not getting any easier. My husband and I were unable to have simple conversations because the spirit of rejection that operated in our lives made it difficult for us to communicate. To know us now, you might wonder how this could be true, but it was. To give you a brief tour into the begining of our married life, one thing that truly affected me was my husband's attitude towards women; he did not respect my position as a woman, as his wife, or as a mother. He has often admitted from the pulpit that this is true of himself, but now, he is a totally different man. When he finally understood the importance of the woman's role in the family, society, and in the church, he became my strongest supporter; today, he works very hard at encouraging women to live up to God's design for their lives.

However, going back to the beginning of our marriage, it was hard for me to accept his mentality about women. I did not know how to react to his attitude towards me and so I remained quiet (if you can imagine that!); I never insisted on defending my rights or my position. Please know this: When we decide to stay quiet and not defend our personal rights, the sovereignty of God descends and makes the necessary changes and adjustments in our lives. Today, Guillermo recognizes that during our first years together, he did not allow me to take my proper place within our marriage and that his attitude was wrong. Now, the story of our relationship is completely different because the Lord taught him where I belonged as a woman, a wife, a preacher, and a prophet. I did not earn my position by fighting or clawing my way up the ladder, but by remaining quiet, humble, and by allowing God to work things out in him and in me. The Lord clothed me with grace and favor before my husband's eyes during those moments of trial and tribulation. Because I understand what it feels to be a woman with passion and destiny and because of my experiences, I am motivated to call forth every woman, especially those in ministry, to tell them with conviction and with certainty:

"Woman of God, you have a calling, but your place is not won by demanding your rights, but rather, by allowing God to work things out on your behalf. Therefore, never surrender; continue in prayer and in faith because God is sovereign — He will lift you up in due season!"

High Adventures...

If a marriage, a baby, and a husband who was a traveling evangelist did not seem enough of a challenge, my husband and I decided to host our own Christian radio program. We inquired at High Adventures Radio Station where we had our first radio broadcast called "Christ is the Answer;" we started this ministry with our pastor's blessing. This was not a local broadcast; it was a program that was heard throughout 70 nations across Central and South America. We paid for our air time with much sacrifice, and each time we felt like giving up, we would read the letters that people sent in. Those letters confirmed that the program was a great blessing to everyone who heard it; we could feel God standing by our side while we struggled to reach the lost. The letters we received came from Mexico, Cuba, Chile, Argentina, Colombia, Venezuela, and many other places. We were especially encouraged by the letters written by pastors who were contemplating leaving the ministry, but who repented and decided to continue serving when they heard the messages over the airwaves. These letters ministered to our life so much that we understood that there were people out there in worse situations than ours. God started to build our ministry as we saw the great need for God's Word in others.

Should We Start a Church?

The days came and went as Guillermo continued traveling to the nations while I served faithfully in the Sunday school ministry at our church. Our son Bryan and I were the only people and moral support that Guillermo could count on. As for me, Bryan was my only friend and constant companion because Guillermo was always too busy with work, the ministry, and his evangelistic travels. For the next nine years, the Lord tested our faithfulness in our marriage, in our finances, in our pride, and in every area of our lives. He tested us in much the same way that He tested the people of Israel during their years in the desert — He uprooted from our lives what needed to be eliminated and allowed circumstances to occur that made us dependant on Him more each day. We shed many tears in the process of God's dealings with us, but we matured. As we look at our ministry and how it is touching lives around the world, it is easy to understand why God allowed these trials and tribulations into our lives; Guillermo and I needed to grow and mature in certain areas in preparation for what was coming concerning the ministry.

We were tested in the area of our finances. I did not have a work permit, and Guillermo struggled to provide for our family while he continued to travel in missionary trips — nothing was going to stop the purpose of God for our lives. Many people become confused and distressed because of their legal status and give up and abandon God's plans, but I am a living testimony of God's abundant grace — it overflows in everyone who is willing to trust in His never-ending mercy and provision. While I cannot deny the fact that we did suffer through difficult situations while we waited for our legal status to change, we never gave up. I worked day and night because it was my salary that paid for the radio programs — canceling these programs was not an option for us.

There were times when our income was only enough to pay the rent, but this never prevented us from faithfully giving our tithes and offerings. Today, we have everything that we need thanks to

God's abundant provision, but we had to pay a very high price to reach the status that we richly enjoy today. Many people see our glory, but they fail to know our story — they have not understood the concept of "reaping what you sow." For many years, we sowed into other people the seeds of prayer, service, fidelity, perseverance, faith, and finances. For this reason, today we are able to honestly declare that we are not in need of anything.

Do not wait to sow during times of abundant harvest; sow at all times. When everyone around you experiences hardship and drought, you will be enjoying the abundant harvest because of your planted seed in due season. The Lord always gives us strength when we are weak if we are willing to put our hands to work. After 13 years of living in the United States without legal documentation, Guillermo and I were able to resolve our legal situation through a federal law that was passed — today, we are United States citizens.

The process that we went through helped us to understand that there was a strong calling in our lives, but we were clueless as to how to develop it; we thought about starting a church, but we did not want to cause division in our own church. We were sure that if we opened a church some people would choose to follow us. We prayed and waited on God until the Apostle Ronald Short — a wonderful man of God who was always watching over us and giving Guillermo the advice that he needed, confirmed what God had already put into our hearts to do; he said that we should leave our church and wait on God to tell us when the time was right to open our own church.

When I think back on the nine years that we spent at that church, I have nothing but good memories to share. We witnessed a beautiful testimony in our pastor; he was a man of integrity in his finances and in his marriage. They helped us organize our wedding with much love and when Bryan was born, theirs was the most beautiful bouquet of flowers that we received. These wonderful expressions of love marked my life forever; I am truly thankful for them.

Our radio ministry was growing rapidly and the Lord quickened our steps; my husband and I were working hard to keep up with what the Lord was doing in us. As we worked, the Lord impregnated us with the magnitude of the vision in reaching the lost. Often, I found myself behind the scenes supporting my husband with prayer when he preached. It was then that I started to have visions; the Lord showed me a church and the multitude. On different occasions, while driving, I noticed how the spiritual realm would open up before my eyes and I was able to see nations before me — God was showing me that He was about to give us a church.

Like I said, God's dealings with us were fast-paced, yet, He only revealed His plan for us one step at a time. First, He gave us a radio program. Second, He gave us an answer to our question about the church. Third, He gave us the people. When we were financially able to finance another radio program, we went to the 1080 AM radio station; from there, we aired our program which was heard at one o'clock in the morning. After each program, we had to minister people who were contemplating suicide or who were experiencing terrible marital problems; some days, we were on the phone with the people until two or three in the morning — apparently that was the time when every problem imaginable became unbearable for people to deal with. The overwhelming response to the radio program was the training ground for our pastoral calling because our passion to minister the people increased with each passing day. The radio programs were never interrupted; not when Guillermo was traveling nor when it seemed that we could not meet the financial responsibility. We sacrificed many things to keep the radio programs going, including time with each other and quality time with our son. Like I said before, Bryan was my constant companion; he also paid the price of serving in the ministry because when Guillermo was traveling, I had to take him with me to the radio station to continue with the program. As difficult as those days were for our family, the ministry and calling that God had placed in our lives were our priority, and we never excused ourselves from the challenges that we had to face in order to obey God.

We worked and served 24 hours a day with the solid conviction that God was in total control and that someday we would see the fruit of our labor. When we learn to trust God in every aspect of our lives, He sees us through every obstacle and challenge; giving up was never an option for us. We were not disappointed because we knew that God was using us in powerful ways to bless the people who heard our programs. This was confirmed by the many letters and phone calls that we received in response to the program; I believe that these letters were the tools that God used to instruct and equip me with the compassion and love for the people who desperately needed answers to their empty and complicated lives. The program and the letters helped me identify myself with the suffering people in Miami and with their personal struggles, with the people who were in need of hope, and with the young ladies who thought suicide was the only way out. As we ministered to the people over the airwaves, we were filled with the passion to establish our own church ministry.

As busy as we were serving, counseling, and ministering others, we continued to struggle with our marriage; this was the hardest area in our lives to overcome. Our personalities and temperaments were completely opposite; we were worlds apart! I was an introvert, a radical, and a shy, fault-finding melancholic. On the other hand, Guillermo was sanguine; to him, everything was a joke and a reason for laughter. With the difference in our personalities, it was very hard for me to align myself with him. I remember crying out to God, "Lord, I don't think he was the right man for me. He and I are incompatible," but God chose to bring us together and to place in our hearts a great vision. As we faithfully served the Lord through the radio program, we were also faithful in our marriage covenant. The one thing that sustained us through it all was the love and the fear of the Lord that never left us. Sometimes, it is hard to understand how we ended up together and married; this is truly a miracle of God because neither of us met the requirements needed for a successful marriage. Nevertheless, the Lord continued to align everything in our daily walk according to His will. I am not saying it was easy, but the Lord gave us the victory.

"²¹Well done, good and faithful servant; you were faithful over a few things, I will make you ruler over many things." Matthew 25.21

Finally, we received the confirmation from the Lord to leave our house of worship — this was a necessary step prior to establishing our own church. We said our good-byes to the pastor, but not before training new leaders to continue the work in the ministerial areas that we were serving in at the time of our departure. Upon arrival at the other church, we were welcomed by the pastor; a very special man of God — he was like a father to us. We did not waste any time when we arrived at this new church, for soon after, we started to inquire of the Lord what area of ministry He wanted us to serve in; His answer to me was: "I want you to work with the children and to clean the bathrooms" and that is precisely what I did. One year later, God spoke to us, and once again, He directed us to leave the church. When we told our pastor how we felt, he confessed that he did not want to see us leave, but we knew that we had to align ourselves with God's will. Because we understand the importance of spiritual covering, we did not want to leave the church without the pastor's blessing. Once again, we spoke with him; this second time he completely understood how we felt and agreed to send us with his blessings. This was the beginning of El Rey Jesus International Ministry and the birth of our son Ronald.

The Birth of El Rey Jesus International Ministry and my Second Son Ronald

When we left the church, we had a vision of what God wanted us to do: to establish El Rey Jesus church. Our first worship service was held in the living room of our home with a total of 12 people, including ourselves. The attendance for each service grew quickly; it was like a bomb had exploded in our living room. God's presence was with us every step of the way as El Rey Jesus continued to grow. When our living room proved too small for our weekly services, Guillermo inquired about space in a shopping center where a telemarketing company and a center for acupuncture had its installations. We were offered the last

remaining available "hole" on the premises where approximate-
ly 30 people would fit, and we took it. The struggle to move the
church from our house into the shopping center was great, but
it was precisely this struggle that motivated me to begin the
ministry of intercession at five o'clock in the morning. The church
was growing rapidly, but along with its membership, the opposition, persecution, and slander also grew. Instead of things getting
easier, they seemed to be going from bad to worse; we were so
busy moving into our new facilities and establishing the various
departments withing the church, including the five o'clock prayer
ministry, that Guillermo and I decided not to take any chances
of getting pregnant again and made an appointment with our
doctor to see how we could permanently prevent this from
happening. The doctor was not pleased with our idea and was
completely against it; according to him, we were too young to
make such a decision because perhaps we would regret it later.
We assured him that our decision had been made and he had
no choice but to comply. During the routine examination prior
to the procedure that would end any possibility of a second
pregnancy, the doctor performed the necesary tests and exam-
inations which concluded that I was very healthy and also five
weeks pregnant. Needless to say, neither of us expected such
news which took us completely by surprise.

Between the church and the usual symptoms of pregnancy, I
started to feel as if we were suddenly under attack on all sides,
but I had already made up my mind that nothing was going to
stop what the Lord had started.

During my pregnancy, I would be at church everyday at five
o'clock in the morning to pray. I would cry out to the Lord:
"Lord, I am afraid of making a mistake." I was truly afraid because
everything that was ahead seemed too difficult to accomplish,
but the Lord spoke to me. I clearly heard Him say: "Wake up
early in the morning and start praying." This was not an easy
request to obey; it cost me many tears.

It is not easy to be a mother of a small child and to also be pregnant, working, and attending a new church ministry. The physical

wear and tear on my body reached its limits. Seven months into the pregnancy, the doctor informed me that I was having contractions and restricted all physical activity; I was not allowed to do anything except lie in bed. I must admit that although I am a firm believer in submitting to authority, I completely disregarded my doctor's orders because I never gave up the prayer ministry. I was faithfully at church every day at five in the morning, rain or shine, and when Guillermo was traveling, Bryan would also join me. When God places a burden in our hearts for His people, the devil will try every scheme imaginable to stop us from fulfilling God's will; that is when we must decide whether to push forward and trust God or drown in a sea of insecurities and excuses. I have never backed down from a challenge and I was not about to start. I took good care of myself during those last two months of pregnancy, but I never gave up what I consider to be the oxygen of our ministry — the prayer ministry.

The early morning intercession ministry was birthed during this trying time; I found refuge in prayer. Through prayer, the Lord started to show me the dangers that drew near the ministry, against my children, and my marriage. Every time I felt that my marriage was threatened, I was able to tell the enemy: "You will not touch my marriage!" Every day, I saw the mercy of God operating in every area of my life; I was also criticized and often treated as if I was crazy; well, if truth be told, I have often been regarded as abnormal. Today, I walk to church every day, hours before the sun rises, with a long wooden stick in one hand, and the sword of the Spirit in the other, praying and taking by force the blessings of the Lord.

The Lord equipped me for prayer and taught me more each day as I learned to hear His voice with clarity. I remember that God spoke to me one day saying, "In the same way that I gave the earth to Adam and Eve to have lordship over it, in that same way, I give you lordship over El Rey Jesus Church. Everything that you allow the enemy to do, I will also allow, and everything that you allow Me to do, I will do. There are only two sources from which you can draw from, the enemy or Me. If you seek My presence, My kingdom, and My will, I will honor the desires of your heart. If you open doors to the enemy, then it shall be done accordingly." My response to the Lord was, "We will not give the enemy anything; not an inch or a particle of dust." I also said, "Lord, I ask that you make me strong and powerful enough to hold the devil under my feet everyday of my life."

Prayer can do great things besides keep the devil under our feet; it can create wonderful miracles as well as establish solid ministries. With El Rey Jesus on its way and the prayer ministry established, it was time to drive to the hospital to welcome our new son — I wanted to name him Guillermo, but my husband was not in complete agreement with me; before we arrived at the hospital, we had both decided that his name would be Ronald, after Ronald Short, a wonderful man of God who has been like a guiding light in our walk with the Lord.

This is the story of how *El Rey Jesus International Ministry* began. It started with twelve people in the living room of my house and now it has multiplied to thousands. It is impossible to speak of the ministry unless prayer is mentioned first; this ministry is founded on prayer.

From Prayer to Warfare...

One day, while standing in front of my closet feeling sad and hurt by the endless situations that we were facing in the ministry and the marital conflicts that Guillermo and I had to deal with, I cried out to the Lord: "Lord, I give up, I am packing my clothes and taking my child away from this place because I cannot take living like this any more; it is too much for me. I want to go where no one can ever find me."

The moment I told the Lord, "I am packing my clothes and leaving," He answered back, "Yes, pack and leave, but know that your decision is exactly what the devil wants you to do. What I want you to do is to stand up and fight." Suddenly, a burst of power exploded on the inside of me. I closed the door to my bedroom and entered into the most impressive time of spiritual warfare that I had ever experienced. I felt fire fall upon me. I remember that on this particular day I had visitors at the house, but that did not matter. Alone, locked in my bedroom, I challenged Satan. I boldly declared; "You are not going to destroy my marriage!"

When the Lord said, "That is what the devil wants to see happen, and if you allow it, there is nothing I can do to stop it. I have given you everything you need to fight him: My Word, My blood, My power, and My name; those things are the equivalent of a spiritual atomic bomb. The question is, 'Do you want to use it or do you want to waste it?' It's your choice. Go ahead, pack your clothes and leave, but remember this, when you go, you will be aborting my plan for your life." When the Lord finished speaking these words into my spirit, I replied, "No Lord, I am not going to let this happen to me." That day I told Satan: "Now hear this Satan, from this day forward, I stand against you with the Lord by my side; my nails are sharpened and I know how to use them against you." I lost track of time. I yelled and fought for hours, and when I walked out of my room, everyone looked at me as if I had gone stir crazy.

That day, alone in my bedroom, the Lord empowered me with an incredible surge of strength as I enlisted to fight in the war against the wicked forces of evil. In the beginning, I was naive about spiritual warfare strategies — much like a soldier who graduates from boot camp and is immediately placed in the battlefield. I had no idea how to fight the war. My only source of reference until that day, concerning such matters, had been the Bible. I had read the Bible enough to know that it contained prayer guidelines, fasting directions, and other ingredients that were needed to fight the good fight, but it was God who showed me how He strategically placed His angels to work alongside of us to work as a team. The Lord also showed me how to set into motion the wheel of creation. Remember, it is in our tongue that we have the power to mobilize demons and angels. One of the first messages that God gave me had to do with the priorities of a Christian, which include: commitment, perseverance, and discipline, among others.

Once I understood these priorities, I decided that God, and my relationship with Him, was my first priority. Because of my decision, the Lord encouraged me to wake up early everyday, before daybreak, and seek His presence. He said to me that what I needed to sustain me through what lay ahead in my life would only be found in Him. The Lord said: "You must take what you need from me in order to overcome what is ahead. In Me, you will find what you need to protect the man of God that stands by your side and the ministry that I have entrusted into your hands. Wake up before sunrise, and I will teach you. I, the Holy Spirit, will be your teacher and show you what you need. I will equip you for war and prepare you to penetrate the devil's defenses. I will show you how to stand against him and how to destroy his plans before they materialize against the ministry." After this, every time that Guillermo prepared to preach, I prayed for him for at least on hour. The results were astronomical!

The Bible teaches that God seeks true worshippers who will worship Him in spirit and in truth. A worshipper is one who spends all of his time in prayer; likewise, to pray without ceasing, one must be a worshipper. Worship and prayer always go together because it is through worship that the Holy Spirit comes upon us to direct our paths.

When we become the kind of worshipers that the Lord is seeking, we also increase our authority on earth and in heaven. The worshipper understands what is happening in the spiritual realm and in the natural realm. When we reach that level of communion with the Holy Spirit, He takes us into heavenly places where we can exercise our authority to bind and loosen. It is there that the Lord says, "Go right ahead and order the principalities, the demons, and the strongholds, the heavens and the earth, the sun and the moon, what they have to do. You have that authority because you are in my presence."

Do you want to be promoted into higher levels of intercession? Do you want to advance from prayer into warfare? If your answer is yes, then you need commitment, perseverance, discipline, and a lifestyle of righteousness and integrity. Bear in mind, living in righteousness does not mean that you have reached the level of perfection, but it does mean that you are now at the point of hating what God hates and loving what God loves.

Thank You Jesus...

I will never cease to thank my Lord for all that He has done in my life. Today, as I look back into my past, I am able to recognize that my Savior's powerful hand was always there to protect me, to watch over me, and to guide me. For this, and for much more, I love Him and I want to serve Him every day of my life. Since the day that I met Jesus, I have learned that every crisis and storm in our lives can either be stumbling blocks to destruction or stepping stones to victory — as long as we learn to trust Jesus. He stands by our side and gives us the victory; He heals every wound and painful memory; He restores our hope and gives us a future; He takes our pain and turns it into testimonial trophies for His glory!

Thanks to my Lord Jesus Christ who saved and healed my broken heart, and thanks to the power of prayer and warfare, I won the battle against fear, shame, unforgiveness, and rejection. These are wonderful victories that I boldly testify every day of my life, but the greatest victories won were the salvation of my parents, my brothers and sisters, and the protection of my home and family.

In time, as the Lord helped my husband and I to mature and grow in the fear of the Lord, we were able to defeat every obstacle in our marriage; we are now living the best moments of our lives. Every year that passes, our marriage grows stronger. The victory was costly, but that is precisely what makes us love our family more, and of course, there should never be any doubt that our marriage is one that was united by God.

I could have chosen to sit and cry my way through the hard times; I could have allowed the enemy to destroy my home, but praise God those were not my choices. I had the strength to confront and face the enemy head on, and in the name of Jesus, rescue my home, fulfill my calling, and bring forth our children and ministry.

If you notice similarities between you and me; if you discover, as you read this book, that you are still carrying the burden of unforgiveness and painful memories that are holding you back; if you still have battles to fight, then now is the time for you to take hold of these words and make them yours. Learn from my testimony of how God took a hurting and innocent little girl and turned her into a woman filled with joy and the love of Jesus; a woman who now has the ability to go forth in the name of Jesus and restore those who are also hurting.

God transformed me. He held an introvert in His hands and shaped me into a preacher, and if He did it for me, then He can also do it for you. It is not a coincidence that you are reading this book. Make every word your own. Learn to fight like a Godly warrior and begin to claim for yourself the blessings that God has for you. This will not be an easy task, but if you trust Jesus and if you are willing to overcome the three enemies that you have to face everyday — the world, the devil, and the flesh — and allow the Holy Spirit to guide you as you surrender to Him your weakness, and crucify your flesh, then one day soon you will be able to declare that you have stepped over from prayer into war. You will never accomplish this in your own strength, but in the strength of the Lord.

To Him is all the glory!

"27... but God has chosen the foolish things of the world to put to shame the wise, and God has chosen the weak things of the world to put to shame the things which are mighty; 28and the base things of the world and the things which are despised God has chosen, and the things which are not, to bring to nothing the things that are, 29that no flesh should glory in His presence." I Corinthians 1.27-29

CHAPTER III

THE ARMOR
OF THE LORD

Soon after my salvation, the devil came against me with full force. His strategy was aimed at trying to make me walk away from the Lord's plans for my life. I remember one day, while in my room, I was attacked by an unseen force that felt like demons were trying to suffocate me; I tried shouting: "In the name of Jesus..." but they would not let me go. I fell to the floor unable to move. I tried to think of what to say because I wanted what was happening to stop; I could not understand why my words were ineffective against that unseen force. I remember thinking why the phrase: "In the name of Jesus" had not worked. Could it have been that I lacked the authority to pronounce them? And then the answer came into my spirit; it is not the words that we speak but the authority that we speak them with; and so I tried it again and said: "In the name of Jesus and by the blood of Jesus, the Son of God." Those simple words were enough for that unseen force to loosened their grip and leave. After that shaky experience, I understood that the reason nothing happened when I said, "In the name of Jesus," was because I still did not trust Jesus completely. I found myself on new ground where I needed to understand the true power and authority that we have in His name; once we receive this revelation in our spirits, the confessions of our mouths will become powerful and effective.

Many Christians live in defeat because they do not know what the Word of God has for them. His Word should not be taken religiously; it is not just good reading material. We must read the Word and meditate on what it says; we must apply it to our lives and live according to its instructions. When the Word becomes real in our lives, it turns into a powerful weapon. Once we learn to live according to the Word of God, to use the weapons of warfare, and to dress ourselves with the Armor of the Lord, there will be nothing that can stop us and no evil that can destroy us.

> "*10Finally, my brethren, be strong in the Lord and in the power of His might. 11Put on the whole armor of God, that you may be able to stand against the wiles of the devil. 12For we do not wrestle against flesh and blood, but against principalities, against powers, against the rulers of the darkness of this age, against spiritual hosts of wickedness in the heavenly places. 13Therefore take up the whole armor of God, that you may be able to withstand in the evil day, and having done all, to stand. 14Stand therefore, having girded your waist with truth, having put on the breastplate of righteousness, 15and having shod your feet with the preparation of the gospel of peace; 16above all, taking the shield of faith with which you will be able to quench all the fiery darts of the wicked one. 17And take the helmet of salvation, and the sword of the Spirit, which is the word of God; 18praying always with all prayer and supplication in the Spirit, being watchful to this end with all perseverance and supplication for all the saints— 19and for me, that utterance may be given to me, that I may open my mouth boldly to make known the mystery of the gospel..."*
> *Ephesians 6.10-19*

When we apply these verses to our lives, we should understand that Paul was describing the image of a Roman soldier; and the reason why we need to wear the armor of the Lord is because we are soldiers in God's army who must fight the war against the forces of evil. The Lord's Armor should never be worn with arrogance but with humbleness before the presence of God.

The body of Christ needs to develop a strong relationship and communion with God; intimacy with the Father empowers us to trust in His protective armor and to accept it as something that is literally real. We should never view the Armor of the Lord as some kind of religious good luck charm; instead, we need to understand that Christ is not dead. He lives in us, and if we understand this basic truth, we will live with the conviction that we are anointed Christians. Jesus is the Great Anointed One, and you and I are the little anointed ones. We are not the living dead because the life of God flows through us. It is our obligation to believe it and to assume His authority. We are the body of Christ on earth and in charge of causing chaos against the wicked forces of evil. The Armor, God's Word, and the name of Jesus are the weapons of our warfare! We must learn to take our position in Christ and discern Satan's plans of attack against the believers in order to take strategic action. Many believers accept that Christ redeemed us at the cross, but this truth is an eternal reality that must be confessed daily. We must take defensive action against the enemy. Jesus was very clear when He said:

> "*[17]And these signs will follow those who believe: in My name they will cast out demons; they will speak with new tongues; [18]they will take up serpents; and if they drink anything deadly, it will by no means hurt them; they will lay hands on the sick, and they will recover." Mark 16.17, 18*

If we believe, the signs will follow! The Word of God that you just read is a promise that belongs to us. We are God's people, and as such, we have to wake up from our spiritual slumber, pick up our spiritual weapons and break through the enemy's territory and take back what belongs to us. The victory is ours because the Word teaches that we are more than conquerors in Jesus Christ our Lord!

We must take our position in the front line of the battlefield; if we do not, the Lord will make us responsible for not praying for our family. He also makes us responsible for allowing the enemy to steal the spoils of war away from us when we do not accomplish His plan and purpose in our lives. We have to wear the Armor of the Lord and to read His Word which is our defensive and offesive weapon of warfare. When we dress ourselves with His armor, we are able to speak to the enemy with boldness and authority; we can remind him that the Word says, "The Spirit of the Lord is upon me; therefore, loosen my family and everything else that belongs to me — enough is enough! You will not take my children or my home; you will not touch my finances or destroy my ministry..."

Make the Word of God your own and fight for the blessings that God has for you. Be aggressive against the devil and order him to: "Let go of my blessings and leave in the name of Jesus!" That is exactly what I had to do when the devil's attacks were stocking up against my family, the ministry, and me. I did not run away; I locked myself in my bedroom and boldly and fearlessly told the devil: "Listen carefully devil, you will loosen and let go of my ministry, now!" I was relentless that day — I felt the power of the name of Jesus behind me; this was a face-to-face fight against the devil, and I was not about to surrender. The Word that was stored in my spirit began to pour from my lips with a powerful force because I had understood its power and my authority in the name of Jesus; God's Word was mine to use against the forces of evil.

> *"[32]It is God who arms me with strength, and makes my way perfect. [33]He makes my feet like the feet of deer, and sets me on my high places. [34]He teaches my hands to make war, so that my arms can bend a bow of bronze. [35]You have also given me the shield of Your salvation; Your right hand has held me up, Your gentleness has made me great. [36]You enlarged my path under me, so my feet did not slip. [37]I have pursued my enemies and overtaken them; neither did I turn back again till they were destroyed. [38]I have wounded them, so that they could not rise; they have fallen under my feet."*
> *Psalms 18.32-38*

The Word that you just read is a powerful declaration of God's love for you. He does not send you into war unarmed; He clothes you with His strength and leads the way to victory; He teaches you to fight and to make war; He is your shield of protection and salvation; He makes you to stand fearlessly before the enemy and destroys the enemy before you. Take His Word today and make it real in your life. My hands, and yours, are trained to pull out and destroy the plans of the wicked one. He equips us to make the devil our footstool and to keep him under our feet. Unfortunately, many people have yet to understand and take hold of these truths and promises found in the Word, and because of it, they are held under the devil's foot instead of the other way around.

My friend, the decision is yours to make. What are you doing with the blessings that God promised to give you? You must go on the offensive and begin to tell yourself: "I will do whatever God tells me to do." You must take authority in your own hands and tell the devil, "You have to loosen and let go of my ministry. I will preach the Word because God trains my hands for war. God teaches me to destroy cancer and poverty; to take my children back from your grip and to destroy every wicked plan that you have devised against God's people." God did not create us to live in poverty and wretchedness. God called His people to victory. Do not worry; do not fret; your victory is near. Do not be afraid; be diligent and wait for the opportunity to blossom — early in the morning.

> *"11Moreover the word of the LORD came to me, saying, "Jeremiah, what do you see?" And I said, "I see a branch of an almond tree." 12Then the LORD said to me, "You have seen well, for I am ready to perform My word." 13And the word of the LORD came to me the second time, saying, "What do you see?" And I said, "I see a boiling pot, and it is facing away from the north." 14Then the LORD said to me: "Out of the north calamity shall break forth on all the inhabitants of the land. 15For behold, I am calling all the families of the kingdoms of the north," says the LORD; "They shall come and each one set his throne at the entrance of the gates of Jerusalem, against all its walls all around, and*

against all the cities of Judah. ¹⁶I will utter My judgments against them concerning all their wickedness, because they have forsaken Me, burned incense to other gods, and worshiped the works of their own hands. ¹⁷"Therefore prepare yourself and arise, and speak to them all that I command you. Do not be dismayed before their faces, lest I dismay you before them. ¹⁸For behold, I have made you this day a fortified city and an iron pillar, and bronze walls against the whole land— against the kings of Judah, against its princes, against its priests, and against the people of the land. ¹⁹They will fight against you, but they shall not prevail against you. For I am with you," says the LORD, "to deliver you." Jeremiah 1.11-19

"Do not be dismayed" were the words of the Lord for Jeremiah. God was telling him not to be afraid. We cannot allow fear to enter our spirit when we declare God's Word. When we speak His Word, His promises, when we establish them in our lives, we must be unyielding and firm. **To be firm** defines an aggressive attitude towards the enemy; the adversary. We may not know what the enemy is planning against us, but we can stop and destroy his plans before they materialize. Do you remember what I said earlier? He must be under our feet, not the other way around. We must take our place as God's children. We must not allow the enemy to scare and intimidate us any more. We must use our weapons of warfare and line up our cannons against the wicked one because the victory is already ours. The victory is yours in the name of Jesus! Believe it. The victory belongs to you!

This is not a war for cowards but a face-to-face combat between God's children and the defeated foe. The people of Israel, in the Old Testament, were in constant battle against the enemy, but their Commander and Chief always went before them; trust your General of War and stretch your hand and penetrate the spiritual realm; appropiate for yourself the redeeming work of Jesus Christ, if you dare. Begin by saying: "Lord, I boldly declare to believe your Word, and right now, I embrace what belongs to me by faith." If you confess this simple statement, you will begin to see changes in your life and in your family; everything around you will begin to change and shine brightly. This change will begin to take place when you trust God and His promises — they are yours for the taking. If you dare to make this decision and enter into war to conquer and destroy, then do not back down — never surrender to the threats of the enemy and always trust God to see you through until the end.

The word **resist** has to do with keeping guard over a piece of land because the enemy roams around like a roaring lion seeking land to seize and conquer. Perhaps, the enemy has been mining your territory and you have been unaware of his deceptions. For this reason, you must maintain an aggressive attitude and decide to seize and conquer first. Never allow the enemy to take what belongs to you! For instance, your fighting, complaining, and outbursts of jealousy between you and your spouse will not solve the problem. Instead, fall on your knees; spend time with God alone and fight. Take back what belongs to you from the world and from the devil. Trust in the Armor of the Lord and in the name of Jesus. Do not allow anyone to take what is rightfully yours. Your fight is not against your spouse, the secretary, or neighbor. Stop blaming others for your problems and conquer the spiritual realm; attack with the weapons of warfare that are at your disposal. Use your sword — the Word of God — against your real enemy, the one who came to rob, kill, and destroy. Attack your true enemy with the authority that belongs to you in the name of Jesus. Remember this, the Son of God came into this world for this very reason, to destroy the works of the devil.

Do not allow the enemy to take what is rightfully yours — that which God has promised you. Continue to sow, to plant, and to trust because it is only by faith and patience that we inherit our promises. God gave us weapons of warfare that guarantee our victory. Now, go out there and fight! Do not allow the enemy to mine, undermine, or destroy your territory.

> *"4But you, brethren, are not in darkness, so that this day should overtake you as a thief. 5You are all sons of light and sons of the day. We are not of the night nor of darkness. 6Therefore let us not sleep, as others do, but let us watch and be sober. 7For those who sleep, sleep at night, and those who get drunk are drunk at night. 8But let us who are of the day be sober, putting on the breastplate of faith and love, and as a helmet the hope of salvation. 9For God did not appoint us to wrath, but to obtain salvation through our Lord Jesus Christ, 10who died for us, that whether we wake or sleep, we should live together with Him. 11Therefore comfort each other and edify one another, just as you also are doing."*
> *1 Thessalonians 5.4-11*

You must be able to see what is going on during the day; therefore, trust His guiding light. *"Your word is a lamp to my feet and a light to my path."* We are not children of the night but children of light and peace, and this requires that we clothe ourselves with the shield of faith and love.

> *"4Love suffers long and is kind; love does not envy; love does not parade itself, is not puffed up; 5does not behave rudely, does not seek its own, is not provoked, thinks no evil; 6does not rejoice in iniquity, but rejoices in the truth; 7bears all things, believes all things, hopes all things, endures all things. 8Love never fails. But whether there are prophecies, they will fail; whether there are tongues, they will cease; whether there is knowledge, it will vanish away."*
> *1 Corinthians 13.4-8*

These verses on love are very important for us to know because they remind us, once more, that our fight is not against our brothers and sisters, but against our enemy who constantly tries to destroy God's love in us. When we speak of love, and everything that love entails, we sadly realize that some Christians envy the people who are promoted in the ministry or who are publicly recognized for their efforts. We should never seek to be acknowledged by men; we should wait for our Heavenly Father to be the One to recognize our efforts. Waiting on men to acknowledge what we do will usually disappoint us, but God uses these moments to measure and test the true intentions of our hearts. In other words, God tests us to see if what we do is for Him or to please a specific individual. If we feel hurt because our efforts went unnoticed, and if we are unable to overcome this disappointment, then we become easy prey for the enemy; he will use our negative attitude against us and make us lose our way to God's blessings.

God's children should learn to understand each other. We need to relate to other people and see ourselves in their particular situations instead of using our mouths to criticize their actions. We are God's people; we have the anointing to restore the brokenhearted and to heal the wounded. It is essential that we position ourselves as armor bearers — as one who willingly protects his brother. We need to take a stand against the devil because our fight is never against flesh and blood. If we do not expose and bring to light the enemy and his plans, how will we be able to defeat him? We must reveal his true nature and line up our cannons against him and not against the people around us. If we want what we declare to become a reality, we must love one another, clothe ourselves with faith, and take His armor with trust, confidence, and authority.

> "*12Therefore, as the elect of God, holy and beloved, put on tender mercies, kindness, humility, meekness, longsuffering; 13bearing with one another, and forgiving one another, if anyone has a complaint against another; even as Christ forgave you, so you also must do. 14But **above all these things put on love, which is the bond of perfection.**" Colossians 3.12-14.*

If we do not meet these requirements, the armor of the Lord will not work for us; without it, we will become discouraged and the "spirit of the SCribes" (false doctrine) will defeat us. We must be strong and demonstrate a firm and aggressive attitude. If we relax, the enemy will take the upper-hand and push us back; we will lose what we have. When the enemy finds us discouraged, he will try to destroy who we are and what we have. Do not lie down in defeat; get up in the name of Jesus!

> *"¹¹Put on the whole armor of God, that you may be able to stand against the wiles of the devil. ¹²For we do not wrestle against flesh and blood, but against principalities, against powers, against the rulers of the darkness of this age, against spiritual hosts of wickedness in the heavenly places. ¹³Therefore take up the whole armor of God, that you may be able to withstand in the evil day, and having done all, to stand. ¹⁴Stand therefore, having girded your waist with truth, having put on the breastplate of righteousness, ¹⁵and having shod your feet with the preparation of the gospel of peace; ¹⁶above all, taking the shield of faith with which you will be able to quench all the fiery darts of the wicked one. ¹⁷And take the helmet of salvation, and the sword of the Spirit, which is the word of God."*
> *Ephesians 6.11-17*

Let us briefly define each part of the armor:

The belt of truth
The breastplate of righteousness
The gospel of peace
The shield of faith
The helmet of salvation
The sword of the Spirit

The Belt of Truth

The belt of truth is the first part of the armor that must be worn. We must tighten the truth around us and bind it to our bodies — around our waist — where the whole armor is held together. Truth gives unity and strength to the rest of the armor.

The waist is the seat of power or the character; it is where strength comes from. In the spiritual realm, if truth is not "tightened to our bodies" we can be easily deceived into believing false doctrine (spirit of the Scribes), which can result in grave consequences. The enemy will take advantage of anything that he can use against us to win the war.

The Breastplate of Righteousness

Righteousness is the breastplate or protective piece of the armor that guards our hearts; it is Christ's righteousness which is accredited to us that stops the wrath of the enemy from destroying us; it also strengthens us and fortifies our hearts against the attacks of the enemy. For the breastplate of righteousness to be effective, it is important for us to have good moral character; this is who we truly are. If our character is well defined and founded in Christ, then we will know who we are in Christ, what we are worth, and where we are going. Understanding these things helps to protect our hearts from being hurt; in other words, it protects us from feeling less then who we really are. If you believe in Jesus and your life is one of obedience and righteousness before God, then your breastplate of righteousness will be effective.

The Preparation of the Gospel of Peace

The preparation of the gospel of peace means that we should learn what the Word says and be prepared to live according to what it says; knowledge in His Word enable us to walk the path of faith with boldness regardless of the circumstances. The Gospel of Peace also means to have peace with God, ourselves, and each other. When we walk in peace, we also walk in repentance which is a powerful weapon against temptation to sin. We cannot enter into warfare against the enemy if we are not well prepared. We must learn what the Word of God says about us and what blessings are promised for us before we enlist to fight the enemy; otherwise, the devil will take advantage of our ignorance in the Word and use it against us — as he did with Eve.

The Shield of Faith

What is faith? It is the evidence of things not seen and the substance of things hoped for. Therefore, faith is the title deed that guarantees that we have everything that God promised us, beginning with the benefits of redemption. Faith is the shield that the enemy cannot penetrate; the devil will try to send his darts of temptation against us because he wants to destroy our souls. Faith in God and in His Word is the shield that stops the devil's fiery darts from piercing the breasplate of righteousness — our moral character.

The Helmet of Salvation

> "⁸...putting on the breastplate of faith and love, and as a helmet, the hope of salvation."
> I Thesalonians 5.8.

The helmet of salvation is also the **hope** of salvation which establishes us as God's children; it protects our soul from being tormented by the devil's tactics. The helmet or hope of salvation keeps us trusting God and rejoicing in His saving grace. It gives us the assurance of salvation, whereby shielding our minds from the destructive thoughts that the enemy tries to send into our minds as part of his wicked plan to contaminate our hearts and destroy us.

The Sword of the Spirit

The sword of the Spirit is the Word of God; it is essential that we learn to use this weapon of warfare in order to defeat the enemy. It is the Holy Spirit that makes His Word come alive in us, making it powerful and effective — sharper than a two-edged sword. We can use this weapon offensively or defensively; when the enemy comes against us with tempting thoughts, we should have God's Word engraved in our spirit so that we can tell the devil: IT IS WRITTEN... Christ himself resisted Satan's temptations with:

> *"⁴It is written, 'Man shall not live by bread alone.'. ⁶It is written again, 'You shall not tempt the LORD your God.' ¹⁰Then Jesus said to him, 'Away with you, Satan! For it is written, You shall worship the LORD your God, and Him only you shall serve.'" Matthew 4.4, 6, 10*

The sword of the Spirit is a weapon that should be used wisely. We should never use it to justify our personal agenda; we should use it under the strict direction of the Holy Spirit to bless, affirm, and edify others as well as to destroy the devil's plans devised against us.

If you take time to meditate on these things, you will come to the conclusion that these parts of the armor will protect you from your head to your feet. We should clothe ourselves with this armor every day and trust it to protect us.

Whether we like it or not, the Word of God must be obeyed; we must declare and practice the principles which are found in the Word and allow God to make us dangerous against the enemy.

If we remain passive, the enemy is going to push us back. We will lose what we have. This is the time when our faith will be tested. Has our faith increased or decreased? We must make a commitment with God every day to not look back and to always have a winning attitude.

Another Powerful Weapon is Prayer

We must never "sit back and watch" as the enemy destroys what belongs to us. It is our responsibility to do everything that is within our ability and power to recover what is stolen from us. Prayer is an effective and powerful weapon that can help us accomplish this. We must pray for our pastors and for our nations; otherwise, how will they change if we do not pull the blessings that await us in the spiritual realm and bring them forth into the physical realm, in the name of Jesus?

We must remember our countries of birth in our prayers. If you have experienced the same as I have and if you left your country to live in "a land flowing with milk and honey," it is no excuse to forget the country of your birth. We must learn from Deborah; a woman who defended the people of Israel. As she defended her people, I will defend my country Colombia. If you stand in the gap for your country, and you do it in the name of Jesus, the devil will have no choice but to step back. Deborah stood her ground and fought for her people, and the Lord placed her enemies into her hands.

As God's people, we must take a stand and demand the devil to "stop, in the name of Jesus. Tell the devil: loosen Miami, loosen my country, loosen my neighborhood, and loosen my family. You have to loosen them in the name of Jesus because I declare it and establish it this day." Your prayer must be powerful enough to make the devil run.

> *"⁷For God has not given us a spirit of fear, but of power and of love and of a sound mind."*
> *2 Timothy 1.7*

Notice what happens when the people gather together as one, with one purpose and one mind.

> *"²⁰Now Herod had been very angry with the people of Tyre and Sidon; but they came to him with one accord, and having made Blastus the king's personal aide their friend, they asked for peace, because their country was supplied with food by the king's country. ²¹So on a set day Herod, arrayed in royal apparel, sat on his throne and gave an oration to them. ²²And the people kept shouting, "The voice of a god and not of a man!" ²³Then immediately an angel of the Lord struck him, because he did not give glory to God. And he was eaten by worms and died. ²⁴But the word of God grew and multiplied." Acts 12.20-24*

These verses testify of what can happen when the church joins together in prayer; they joined together to request that God's voice be heard. Their unified prayer caused Herod to be eaten by worms when he decided to persecute the Christian people. This is an important lesson that must be learned: when we pray as one, the Father sends His angels and commands them to act according to His Word that is declared by our confession. The question is not whether God can do it; rather, is the prayer of agreement powerful enough to make things happen? If you are unsure of the authority that you have in Christ, then begin to read Scripture and learn the fullness of what God has entrusted into your hands. Your prayer of agreement, as God's child, will cause definite changes in the city of Miami, or wherever you are because as your prayer penetrates the heavenlies, the Lord sends His angels to act on His Word, which is spoken through you.

When God's children gather together to pray and to cry out as one voice for the nations, our prayers rise before His throne of grace because our Heavenly Father promised to give us the nations as our inheritance. It does not matter that our nation has principalities and strongholds; we will destroy them in the name of the Son of God — in the name of Jesus!

Another very important thing that we must never do is to allow the spirit of fear to intimidate us when we pray. We need to learn to use every resource available to fight for what belongs to us; do not fall behind. Take a strong stand in the name of Jesus and lay claim to what is rightfully ours. Stop complaining! Wear the armor of the Lord and use the weapons of warfare that God has made available to us and watch what happens when we use them without hesitation. Follow in His footsteps knowing that "Jesus is the way." We must enter into warfare with our eyes set on the author and finisher of our faith. We need to tell our Lord, "Here I am, I am going to my neighborhood and to my family." The Lord is seeking men and women like us to declare His word; He wants us to use the power that is in the name that is above all names, the name of Jesus of Nazareth, the Son of God!

Do something! Begin by praying for the servant of God; declare God's protection over his life and establish that the land will be ready for planting. In much the same way that the land is prepared to receive the natural seeds, we must prepare the hearts of the people for the planting of His word by the chosen and anointed servant of God.

> *"¹The Spirit of the Lord GOD is upon Me, because the LORD has anointed Me to preach good tidings to the poor; He has sent Me to heal the brokenhearted, to proclaim liberty to the captives, and the opening of the prison to those who are bound; ²To proclaim the acceptable year of the LORD, and the day of vengeance of our God; to comfort all who mourn, ³to console those who mourn in Zion, to give them beauty for ashes, the oil of joy for mourning, the garment of praise for the spirit of heaviness; that they may be called trees of righteousness, the planting of the LORD, that He may be glorified." ⁴And they shall rebuild the old ruins, they shall raise up the former desolations, and they shall repair the ruined cities, the desolations of many generations. ⁵Strangers shall stand and feed your flocks and the sons of the foreigner shall be your plowmen and your vinedressers ⁶But you shall be named the priests of the LORD, they shall call you the servants of our God. You shall eat the riches of the Gentiles, and in their glory you shall boast. ⁷Instead of your shame you shall have double honor, and instead of confusion they shall rejoice in their portion. Therefore in their land they shall possess double; Everlasting joy shall be theirs." Isaiah 61.1-7*

Make these words your own; they are yours and mine to use. Wear the armor of the Lord and go forth to restore the brokenhearted and to plant trees of justice in the name of Jesus.

CHAPTER IV

THE POWER OF THE WORD

God spoke the word and by the power of His word we were created. Every son and daughter of God must appropriate the power that is found in Scripture when we declare its words. We can speak a "creative word" and make the supernatural of God to manifest in us. God's children have the power to curse or to bless; to build or to destroy our lives and the lives of the people within our sphere of influence. We also have the power to cancel and to destroy anything that dares come against the will of God for our lives. When our words are aligned with God's Word, and when they carry the fullness of the power in the Holy Spirit, we have the assurance that when we speak to the mountain and cast it into the sea in the name of Jesus, it shall be done.

> *"21 So Jesus answered and said to them, "Assuredly, I say to you, if you have faith and do not doubt, you will not only do what was done to the fig tree, but also if you say to this mountain, "Be removed and be cast into the sea,' it will be done. 22 And whatever things you ask in prayer, believing, you will receive."*
> *Matthew 21.21, 22*

Jesus makes Himself very clear in these verses. He said that if we have faith when we speak, whatever we "say" will be done. He did not say to "push the mountain into the sea," He said: "speak to the mountain." How many times, having the power of the "creative word" at our disposal, do we try to "push" the mountain with our own strength instead of "speaking" to it? We try to change things in our own strength when we challenge our spouses or become depressed when we face difficult situations. We easily forget that to create and attract the blessings from heaven into our lives all we need to do is to open our mouths and speak faith-filled words.

When we say, "I can't", it is because we are trying to solve the problem at hand with our own strength and understanding. However, when we humble ourselves and recognize that the Spirit of God is the One who works through us, we will understand that all things are possible. In other words, when we recognize that giving our burdens over to God, and after we speak the right way, we will be blessed and receive that which we hope for. On the other hand, when we confess our inability to accomplish what we want, we instantly become the devil's instrument; he will use our own negative confessions to curse our lives. We are the end result of our spoken words.

It is unfortunate to witness men and women of God confessing negative words and then having to deal with the consecuences of their confessions. They speak negatively because they are yet to be impregnated with the Word of God. They are unable to apply it or to establish it in their lives. For you to be able to use the power of God's Word creatively, it is necessary to believe it and to establish it. When we confess and establish the Word, it becomes rhema in our spirit.

> *"²¹Death and life are in the power of the tongue and those who love it will eat its fruit."*
> *Proverbs 18.21*

The Lord created us with the freedom to choose. Therefore, it is up to us to decide if we are going to speak blessings or curses. We are what we speak, every day of our lives!

Ask yourself, "What do you love most right now?" "What are you constantly saying?" Do the following words sound familiar? "I can't, I have no job, and I am defeated..." Well, here is a newsflash for you. I lived for 13 years in this country illegally and without knowing one word in English. As hard as living like this was for me, I continued to praise God and give Him thanks because I was never out of work. For this reason, and with the authority that I have earned through experience, I can tell you that there is no excuse to say "I can't"; this phrase should be totally eliminated from our vocabulary. It does not belong to the people who believe that God is powerful because the meaning of the word "powerful" implies and declares that He can do all things, and you can do all things in Him if you choose to take His hand.

When my husband and I started in the ministry, a servant of God told me; "Put your hands on this project and support the vision." When we heard these words, we understood that we should continue to pay for the radio program with my income. It was not easy, but I would say to myself every day: "I can do it. Thank you Father for blessings us; I have no doubt that you will provide."

I believed my Father and surrendered completely to the vision. When you want to do something, earn your money by working hard, and the Lord will give and bless you gradually. Do not just sit there complaining about your situation. If you need a job, go into the business world, and begin filling out employment applications, but before you enter any potential workplace, give God thanks for the job that is already yours; the job that He will bless you with and with which you will bless others. If you are having trouble at home, with your spouse or your children, stop complaining and bad-mouthing them, and begin to use the power of the spoken word that is in you to make positive changes in your family. Fast and pray; cry out to your Heavenly Father; shout to the devil that he does not have any authority over your family. Remind the devil that you are God's child and that your word is full of the power and the anointing of the Spirit of God to destroy every stronghold.

From the first day that I received Jesus as Lord, God has led me from one victory after another. I fought for five long years over a very difficult financial situation, but this did not stop me. I decided to confess the Word of God and started to sow for the Kingdom; I stayed on course until the moment when the days were perfected in Him.

God spoke the word, and immediately all things were created; He said: *"Let the waters bring forth abundantly and swarm with living creatures"* and the sea was filled with fish. Words are the bridge between the spiritual and earthly realm. Appropriate yourself with this truth and believe that God's Word is true. Never stop believing that God's blessings belong to you. To receive divine healing for your body, happiness for your home, financial stability, and your ministry, you must believe in the delegated power and authority in your spoken word; God gave it to you to do great things. Grab and hold on to the blessings found in Deuteronomy 28; make them real in your life!

> *"¹Now it shall come to pass, if you diligently obey the voice of the LORD your God, to observe carefully all His commandments which I command you today, that the LORD your God will set you high above all nations of the earth. ²And all these blessings shall come upon you and overtake you, because you obey the voice of the LORD your God: ³"Blessed shall you be in the city, and blessed shall you be in the country. ⁴"Blessed shall be the fruit of your body, the produce of your ground and the increase of your herds, the increase of your cattle and the offspring of your flocks. ⁵"Blessed shall be your basket and your kneading bowl. ⁶"Blessed shall you be when you come in, and blessed shall you be when you go out. ⁷"The LORD will cause your enemies who rise against you to be defeated before your face; they shall come out against you one way and flee before you seven ways. ⁸"The LORD will command the blessing on you in your storehouses and in all to which you set your hand, and He will bless you in the land which the LORD your God is giving you. ⁹"The LORD will establish you as a holy people to Himself, just as He has sworn to you, if you keep the commandments of the LORD your God and walk in His ways. ¹⁰Then all peoples of the earth shall see that you are called by the name of the LORD, and they shall be afraid of you. ¹¹And the*

LORD will grant you plenty of goods, in the fruit of your body, in the increase of your livestock, and in the produce of your ground, in the land of which the LORD swore to your fathers to give you. [12]The LORD will open to you His good treasure, the heavens, to give the rain to your land in its season, and to bless all the work of your hand. You shall lend to many nations, but you shall not borrow. [13]And the LORD will make you the head and not the tail; you shall be above only, and not be beneath, if you heed the commandments of the LORD your God, which I command you today, and are careful to observe them. [14]So you shall not turn aside from any of the words which I command you this day, to the right or the left, to go after other gods to serve them." Deuteronomy 28.1-14

The same way that God spoke and creation was made, we must speak and pull the blessings from the spiritual realm into the physical world. As God's children, we must take His Word and treasure it in our hearts. We must put His Word into action and see the blessings shower into every area of our lives until they "runneth over".

There is power in the word, not the positive word of which the world talks about, but the **Word of God from which all things can be created**. Today, you have the power to change the patterns of behavior that have kept you in poverty and defeat for so long; you can alter the direction of your life by changing the words that you speak. Stop saying: "I can't" and replace them with: "I can do all things through Christ who strengthens me." If you believe what the Word says about you, then believe me when I tell you that you will always be the "head and not the tail." "You will be blessed in your comings and goings." "Everything that your hands touch will prosper, and whatever your feet touch you will possess."

In the name of Jesus, I declare and establish that if you believe and appropriate yourself of what you have read in this chapter, you will never be the same again. Today, you have enlisted to occupy a position of leadership in the Lord's Army.

CHAPTER V

RESTORING THE AUTHORITY DELEGATED BY GOD

God created man in His image and likeness to represent His authority on earth. However, for many of us, that image of authority means very little because the authority that we grew up with, those who were supposed to represent God's authority on earth, abused and mistreated us. This twisted misrepresentation of authority has caused many women to ask themselves, "How can I respect my authority when they have caused me so much pain and suffering?" In this chapter, we will learn what the woman's place is, and what we have to do to lead our men into the place of authority that belongs to them within the home and in the church.

Fallen Authority and Lordship

At times, it is a difficult task for women to restore the spiritual priesthood of men because, in looking back into our childhood and teenage years, the one thing that stands out is pain. There is also pain in the marital relationship because of the extensive abuse caused by the people in our lives that held a position of authority. When we come to Christ we ask ourselves, "How can I respect those in authority?" "What should I do to place myself where God wants me if these people that represent authority have caused me so much pain?" The answers to these questions can only be found in His Word.

Unfortunately, respect for authority is rarely taught at home; after the child grows up and moves out of the house, this lack of respect spills over into the church and the business world. If this type of behavior is not corrected in time, eventually, when boys become men and establish their own families, they will be unprepared to deal with the difficult situations that might arise;

they will be either unable or unwilling to take the responsibility of their families upon their shoulders. For instance, when a child needs to hear words of affirmation or perhaps he has situations that need to be resolved, the father will be absent or too busy to take care of his child's needs.

Most people that I counsel and minister inner healing use expressions such as: "He left me for another woman; I am incapable of dealing with the problems that I am facing today; I left him because he was addicted to pornographic websites." These women, instead of facing their problems, surrender to the enemy and to his demons; this has to change! The correct attitude for these women should have been: "I am going to follow my Lord, my Creator, my God, and I am taking authority and the priesthood that God has given me to destroy the works of the devil." Why is it difficult to walk the Lord's path set for me? We must ask God to break our wills, to make us new, and to help us restore that authority as women, as mothers, and as daughters because God created us to have authority.

> *"27So God created man in His own image; in the image of God He created him; male and female He created them." Genesis 1.27*

This verse confirms that God said, "Let us make man in our image and likeness." At the moment of creation, God the Father, the Son, and the Holy Spirit were present. God said: "Let us give man lordship over creation; he will govern and have authority over every created thing. He will be lord." This place of authority only lasted a short time because sin and damnation entered humanity through Adam's disobedience. If we continue reading the book of Genesis, we will find that the Word of God says:

> *"8And they heard the sound of the LORD God walking in the garden in the cool of the day, and Adam and his wife hid themselves from the presence of the LORD God among the trees of the garden. 9Then the LORD God called to Adam and said to him,* **"Where are you?"** *Genesis 3.8, 9*

"Where Are You?"

The Lord called out to Adam: "Where are you?" He is asking this same question to you right now: "Where are you?" "Man, where are you when your wife is going through difficult times and she needs you to be there for moral and spiritual support?"

There is a cry being heard in the families where the father is absent. Abused, mistreated, and violated children are crying out saying: "Where is my daddy?" "Dad, where were you when I suffered the difficult moments in my childhood and teenage years?" "What was more important than to be by my mother's side when she was pregnant?" "Are you aware that mom had to work very hard to support me?" "Did you know that mom had to deal with her employer's sexual harassment?" "Was this necessary, dad?"

This is the reason why families today are in chaos; why families are destroyed and why we have so many single mothers. **"Where is the man that I created?** This is the question that God is asking Himself these days.

The same question that the Lord asked Adam, He is asking men today: "Where are you?" If Adam had called out to Eve, the way that God called out to Adam, he would have stopped the curse of disobedience from falling upon mankind. The question now is: "Where was Adam and why did he not defend the woman that God gave him?" If Adam had said, "Devil, you will not touch my wife because she was given to me by God to protect and to guard over her. I rebuke you and cast you out..." Had Adam done what God created him to do — to be the protector, the head of the family, the husband, provider, and the emotional giver, we would not have any need for books such as this one. I pray that these simple yet profound words melt your heart away right now!

I am blessed to have received from God a man that is always there for me when I need him. But what happens with the women that are alone and asking God about the men in their lives. "Where are you?" is the same question God asked Adam and today He is asking you, "Men, when your authority is needed in the home, where are you?" "When the bills need to be paid, where are you?" Men, you must remember that you are the priest and head of your home; the provider and the one in charge of the checkbook. In other words, you are responsible for taking care of the financial situation in your home. You must take your position and receive the wonderful blessing that God has given you. We trust that God is going to do something spectacular with the priesthood in His church by confronting those who were created to be in authority. This way the children who are crying out from the depth of their being for a father can begin to count on one, thanks to the order established by God. And these men can begin to say, "Here I am Lord."

God is the beginning or the origin of authority. He is also the One who established order in every area of life. God delegates this authority in different ways and the first that He establishes is the authority in the family.

> *"³But I want you to know that the head of every man is Christ, the head of woman is man, and the head of Christ is God." I Corinthians 11.3*

The Word gives us strength and fortitude to our bones and wisdom to help us stay where God wants us to be in order that we may become a different kind of people; "A holy nation, a royal priesthood, a generation chosen by God." Because of the Word, I want to remind you of the following: Women, submit to your husbands; men, submit to Christ as Christ submits to God. According to this statement, the first authority in our homes is Christ; after Him comes the authority of the men, followed by the woman's authority and last but not least the children. There is also an established order in the church. First, are the pastors, followed by the ministers, the elders, the deacons, and so on.

Authority Established by God

> *"²Therefore whoever resists the authority resists the ordinance of God and those who resist will bring judgment on themselves." Romans 13.2*

There is no government on the face of this earth that God has not allowed to govern. He has delegated authority to those who are in the position of authority, whether it is the president, the mayor, or the police department. It is important to respect these authority figures; otherwise, we will receive our due punishment for disregarding the law.

God established the levels of authority that we need at home, at the church, and in government. For this reason, if we resist what God established, such as the authority of the priesthood and other people in authority, we will suffer terrible consequences. The Word mentions several examples of people who rebelled against the authority established by God or against someone in the position of high priest. To mention just a few, these people include: Miriam, Aaron, Saul, and Aaron's sons. Many more were cursed because of their disobedience and irreverence towards the authority established by God. Let us read the following passage and refresh our memory concerning Miriam and Aaron.

> *"¹Then Miriam and Aaron spoke against Moses because of the Ethiopian woman whom he had married; for he had married an Ethiopian woman. ²So they said, "Has the LORD indeed spoken only through Moses? Has He not spoken through us also?" And the LORD heard it. ³(Now the man Moses was very humble, more than all men who were on the face of the earth.) ⁴Suddenly the LORD said to Moses, Aaron, and Miriam, "Come out, you three, to the tabernacle of meeting!" So the three came out. ⁵Then the LORD came down in the pillar of cloud and stood in the door of the tabernacle, and called Aaron and Miriam. And they both went forward. ⁶Then He said, if there is a prophet among you, I, the LORD, make Myself known to him in a vision; I speak to him in a dream. ⁷Not so with My servant Moses; He is faithful in all My house. ⁸I speak with him face to face, even plainly, and not in dark sayings; and he sees*

> *the form of the LORD. Why then were you not afraid to speak against My servant Moses?" ⁹So the anger of the LORD was aroused against them, and He departed. ¹⁰And when the cloud departed from above the tabernacle, suddenly Miriam became leprous, as white as snow. Then Aaron turned toward Miriam, and there she was, a leper."*
> *Numbers 12.1-10*

The subject on authority is fundamental and delicate. I hope that you are able to apply this basic principle in your life because without it you will go into battle unprotected. Furthermore, disobedience, in its many forms, including rebellion against authority, is an open door to the enemy that gives him legal rights to mine your territory. If you refuse to submit to authority, you will lose your authority before men.

I pray and ask the Lord to raise leaders such as Moses, who are humble and meek and who never see fit to defend themselves — when Moses' wife Zipporah died, he remarried a dark-skin woman; his choice was immediately criticized by Miriam and Aaron, but he did not defend himself. Many people today criticize or judge people in authority because of their race, culture, or skin color; if you are one of those people, be careful because that is an authority established by God and we must respect them.

Perhaps people have judged you because of your skin color; if this happens again remember: dark-skin or not, every son and daughter of the King has blue-blood running through their veins; in the eyes of God, there is no Jew or Greek, no man or woman; we are all the same. God is raising people from different cultures and races including Native Americans and Afro-American leaders precisely because He sees potential in all of us regardless of what we look like on the outside. People who judge others because of their skin color are going to be pleasantly surprised when they arrive in heaven and see those they least expected to find waiting for them. What if the people that they find in heaven are dressed in their Native American ceremonial clothing which barely covers their bodies; what will they say to the Lord: "I'm leaving because heaven is full of natives?" You might find this funny, but I have to confront many people today who are still dealing with this type of racism.

How is it possible that we can resist the authority of God and still speak words that we should never utter? Remember Miriam, Moses' sister? She was humbled, humiliated, and cursed with leprosy before the nation of Israel. She had to leave the camp as an outcast for seven days for criticizing her brother Moses — the man of God. Consider yourself warned next time you feel the urge to criticize the man of God. Be careful because your criticism causes curse and damnation to enter your life; it also causes the plans of God to be delayed. Have you ever asked yourself how many people have caused God's plans to be delayed? God's plans are slowed down by the words of those who are careless to speak and destroy the authority established by God.

I must admit that there have been times in my life when I have not always submitted to authority; when this has occurred, the Lord has revealed it to me, and I have recognized and accepted His discipline and quickly repented. Because I understand how it feels to submit to authority and what it feels like to be disciplined by the Lord when I rebelled against Him, I can say for certain that many people today resist authority but are unaware of their actions.

As women, mothers, and role models we need to do our part and obey. Woman, are you willing to do your part? Are you challenged to do what God has entrusted you to do? If men want to take their rightful place or not, that is not our problem, it is theirs. We are going to do our part! I assure you, my precious sister, that when we pray before the presence of our Heavenly Father He will not hold back anything from us. He answers the prayers of a mother, a young woman, or a wife who cries out in His presence. God opens the heavens and pours out His blessings in abundance when we approach His throne with humbleness. He not only opens the windows but also the doors of heaven to manifest Himself in favor of His church and of His beloved people that were redeemed with His Son's blood. We must take a stand and pray so that authority can be restored in our homes.

If we choose to live in a foreign country that speaks a language that is unknown to us, we must learn to speak that language in order to communicate. The same thing happens when we receive Christ; we become citizens of a different nation, one that speaks a different language. Therefore, we must learn to speak the heavenly language to pray and seek God's presence. We must stop using the world's language and begin to declare God's Word as we take our rightful place as children of the King. We learn to speak a new language and change our lifestyles to learn what it means to be under authority.

If we have a hard time submitting to authority figures, prayer is the answer to our problem. We know that prayer is necessary for every facet of our lives, but we have yet to implement that truth in our daily lives. This is why I am not surprised that in our church of over six thousand active members only a small remnant gathers together to pray. How long will God have to wait for His people to pray for authority to be established, for man to take his place in the divine order of God, and for order to exist in His church?

What an incredible difference in the way that people respond when they are invited to pray and when they are invited to a party! When people are invited to pray, the only people who show up are those who are keenly aware of their priorities, which are few, in comparison to the many people who accept the invitation to an overcrowded party. As God's people, we must change our mentalities. When we are called to pray for our nation, many do not open their mouths to declare the power of God that is readily available to make changes. Instead of blessings, we continually make declarations that destroy. We say such things as: "This country is worthless and rubbish," when we should be saying: "This is the land where God has brought me and He promised to bless me wherever I go." Sometimes I ask myself, "If God's people are aware of the prayer meetings at church that are specific to their needs, including marriage, youth, health, etc, and if their marriages are on the brink of destruction or their children are being led astray by the wrong company they keep, then why are they still unwilling to learn the prayer language and begin to cry out Abba Father? What are people waiting for? When God says, *"If My people who are called by My name would humble themselves, I would forgive their sin and heal their land..."* God is saying, "If my people would only pray and humble themselves, I would heal their families, their marriages, their children..."

We are in need of men with hearts such as Moses' heart in leadership and around us. Moses was a noble and kind leader with the heart of an intercessor. One instant in which he demonstrated his kindness was the time when God punished his sister Miriam for criticizing him; he interceded on her behalf and asked the Lord to heal her body from leprosy. Just as Miriam's criticism caused her to be punished with leprosy, many Christians today are contaminated by spiritual leprosy; they are in poverty because they spoke against their authorities. Some might say, "Who does she think she is, telling me what to do?" Well, if she is in the position of authority, whether you like it or not, you must recognize and accept that she is sent by God, and it is an act of disrespect to question her authority.

Authority Delegated by God

The pastor is the authority delegated by God in the church. The ministers, elders, and deacons are people who execute an authority that is delegated by God through the pastor, and it must be respected and honored; we should not question their position or reject them. We must abort the attitude of those who say, "When I go to the church I only want to deal with the Pastor, if not him..." These types of people do not respect the authority that was delegated to those in charge. Be careful! Remember, it was God who placed them in that position. The same thing happens outside the church, with the police department and other authority figures. Do not lose your perspective. Take a moment to think about how many people are imprisoned at this moment because they resisted authority. This is a sad happening, to hear of the horrific acts that these men, women, and adolescents are guilty of and what they have to suffer behind bars. Their misfortune is the consequence of resisting authority at home, and because they chose not to obey at home, they were unable to respect any outside authority.

In the Old Testament, the Lord sent a message to King Saul through his prophet Samuel saying:

> *"³Now go and attack Amalek, and utterly destroy all that they have, and do not spare them; kill both man and woman, infant and nursing child, ox and sheep, camel and donkey."' I Samuel 15.3*

Saul was instructed to destroy everything, but he did not obey God's command; he spared the life of Agag, king of the Amalekites and the best of the sheep, oxen, fatlings, lambs, and all that was good, though he destroyed the rest of the people. His justification for disobeying God's word was that he spared the best of the sheep and oxen to sacrifice to the Lord. When Samuel heard this, he said: "Why did you not obey the voice of the Lord?"

> *"²²So Samuel said: "Has the LORD as great delight in burnt offerings and sacrifices, as in obeying the voice of the LORD? Behold, to obey is better than sacrifice, and to heed than the fat of rams. ²³For rebellion is as the sin of witchcraft and stubbornness is as iniquity and idolatry. Because you have rejected the word of the LORD, He also has rejected you from being king." I Samuel 15.22, 23*

When Saul heard this, He answered:

> *"²⁴Then Saul said to Samuel, "I have sinned, for I have transgressed the commandment of the LORD and your words, because I feared the people and obeyed their voice. ²⁵Now therefore, please pardon my sin, and return with me, that I may worship the LORD." I Samuel 15.24, 25*

Saul's repentance came a bit too late; this was Samuel's response:

> "*²⁶But Samuel said to Saul, "I will not return with you, for you have rejected the word of the LORD, and the LORD has rejected you from being king over Israel... "²⁸The LORD has torn the kingdom of Israel from you today, and has given it to a neighbor of yours, who is better than you."*
> I Samuel 15.26, 28

Saul disobeyed God's command and the authority that He had placed before him (Samuel); sometimes we disobey by choosing to do something that appears to be a good thing — such as Saul and his sacrifice — but we forget that instead of doing what is good, we should do what is right before God's presence. We cannot do things our way, as Saul did, because it is a sin before God. Therefore, when the leader tells you to do something, do it exactly as he tells you to do it not how you think it should be done. Do you realize that Saul lost his kingdom because of his disobedience? What will we lose if we disobey? Saul was replaced by King David, a man with a different heart, mind, and attitude.

When Saul went after David to kill him out of jealousy, David found out about it and so did his men. David's men urged him to kill Saul while he slept in the cave, but this was King David's answer:

> "*⁶And he said to his men, "The LORD forbid that I should do this thing to my master, the LORD's anointed, to stretch out my hand against him, seeing he is the anointed of the LORD."* I Samuel 24.6

Saul was wrong in his actions, and disobedience caused him the kingdom; it was given to David — hence, his jealousy against David and the reason why he wanted David dead. David might have been justified to kill Saul, afterall, it would have been self-defense, but he knew that he had to behave properly if he wanted God to bless him; David understood that at that moment, Saul was the authority over Israel and that it was his responsibility and act of obedience to respect that authority which was established by God.

We must learn to be like David and respect and obey the authority that God has placed over us. It is extremely important for the fear of the Lord to abide in our lives; this will prevent us from falling into the misconception that we can resist and disobey the authority that has been delegated by God simply because we disagree with their leadership methods.

It is easier to obey a pastor than his wife or another female leader in a position of authority. Some might say, "I want to see the pastor and not his wife." Well, allow me to inform you that if God places a woman in a position of authority, she must also be respected. Authority has nothing to do with gender; it has to do with God and we must obey. If we understand the concept of obedience, submission, and authority then we will be better bondservants of Christ. If we look into our ministries, notice how many people in leadership positions leave their departments without saying a word because they had a problem with authority.

The problem is that too many people feel that they should be granted special honors; they believe that their position gives them the special privilege to resist authority. These people should repent and seek God's forgiveness for resisting authority in their homes, in society, at church, and everywhere they go.

We must continue praying one for the other in respect to our attitude towards authority so that we can remain respectful and obedient to them. In other words, if you resist your husband, your leader, or the people in government, you are resisting God, and people who resist His authority have the same spirit of rebellion operating in their lives that operates in Satan. This is why we must change our language and substitute it for the heavenly language; through prayer, we can root out this evil from our churches and society.

Passiveness

Why did men lose their role as spiritual high priests? — Because of their accommodating attitude. The curse of passivity has operated in men for centuries. To have a passive attitude means not taking action when the family is in crisis. For instance, people who are passive will be encouraged to attend retreats or conferences, but their laid-back attitude makes them postpone the decision to attend for a later time. They will usually answer most invitations with: "Later!" When they are reminded that their utility bills are overdue, again they answer: "Later!" When they are asked to send their children to be baptized, again they answer: "Later!" They are told to bring their children to church so that God can touch them and their answer is: "Later!" These are examples of parents who are passive. Yet, the Word of God tells us to: *"Seek the LORD while He may be found, call upon Him while He is near, because the time is coming when you will seek me and not find me."*

Listen carefully people of God. The time is coming when you will try to find God and not find Him. Now is the time to break away from passiveness and say: "I will be agressive; I will stand up and serve my God. I will walk the path that God has traced for me!" Many people have been told that they are called to the ministry of deliverance, but they do nothing about it. Perhaps, they are told that they have the calling for intercession, but their answer is: "Later, when I stop being afraid and when I am not so lazy." "Later" should not be our answer to God's calling; men must be serious about their role as high priest; otherwise, women will have to take over their place and role in society. Because of lazy and passive men, wives are burdened by the growing financial responsibilites of the home; instead of waiting hopelessly for the day when these men will wake up from their laziness, these women prefer to leave their homes to enter the job market in order to take care of their financial obligations. However, their decision to supply the needs of the family keeps the men passive because they are not given the time that they need to assume their responsibilities as head of the home. The same thing happens when men do not pray; with men who do not attend church and who take for granted their authority and everything that this authority entails. Men force the women in their lives to take over their role as head of household, their responsibilities, and as high priest in their home with their passive attitude. These women say, "If he does not go, then I have to go. If he does not do it, then I will have to make up the difference."

What is the result of passiveness? It prevents men from taking their place as leaders in their homes and it prevents them from taking action when the problems appear. What happens when a man is passive? The woman eventually takes his place. Right now, I want to invite the women who were forced to take over their husband's role as leader in the home, as well as continuing with their roles as women and mothers, to stand up and go into war against the enemy. The devil's plans have always included the destruction and the breakdown of the man's position as high priest, not only in the home, but also in society. Therefore, stand firm and demand the following of the devil, "Loosen my husband. In the name of Jesus, I order every spirit of passiveness to leave his life and my home. I declare that my husband is a man that establishes the lordship of Jesus Christ, just as God ordained it. I declare that from this moment forward, he is my headship, my authority, and I declare that God gives him the wisdom that he needs to execute his authority."

How is it that men can be such cowards as to allow "imps or little demons" to defeat them? Their cowardice forces women to take action and to pray. Women must increase their faith in God; they need to believe that He will touch and encourage their men to take their place as high priests and establish the Lordship of Christ in the home, as it should be. Women received the power, the authority, and the legal right from God to declare that this must be done on earth.

Aggressiveness

We must be aggressive against the enemy at all times. We cannot go to sleep while denying the existence of the devil because he roams around seeking ways to kill and to destroy everything that God created. We must be on guard and ready, waiting for the right time to attack. We cannot afford to stand still while the devil comes after us; instead, we must perceive the place where he might hide and shake his foundation. Speak to the devil with intimidating authority. Say: "Where are you? When I find you, I will root you out and ruin you; I will cast you out and get you out of my home. I will get you out of my finances; I will get rid of you! I have the authority to do it in the name of Jesus. I have God's Word. He has placed it in my mouth to root out, to ruin, and to destroy the works of the devil."

When the person in authority, or the man, has abandoned the home or is away from home for other reasons, the enemy will try to take advantage of that situation. During these times, when the head of the home is away, the women must not allow themselves to be destroyed. Instead, they must rise to the occasion and clothe themselves with valor and with the "strength of a wild ox." Women must learn to execute their authority, in the name of Jesus, and stop the enemy from taking the upper hand in any situation. This is exactly what happened during one of my husband's trips to Honduras. My son Bryan fell ill; his symptoms were fever and vomiting. I did not sit passively while the enemy tried to hurt my child. I quickly took control of the situation, and though I was alone in the house, I held my ground and told the enemy, "You filthy beast, I rebuke you in the name of Jesus." I laid hands on my son and ordered the devil to loosen him. My prayer was answered. The fever and the vomiting disappeared and my son was healed and delivered instantly. On a different occasion, my husband had to attend a convention and again I was left alone. I perceived in the spirit that "they" wanted to hurt me. Therefore, I awoke at around two in the morning and said, "So, this is how it's going to be, ah? Well, this is how I'm going to deal with you, you filthy devil..." I picked up the telephone and called an intercessor and asked her, "Stand in agreement with me because I am a little afraid, but right now, together, we are going to beat this little demon down," and in the name of Jesus, we went into warfare. "How dare you come against me with fear; how dare you try to tempt me when the high priest, the authority, is away from home? I rebuke you and cast you out with the authority that I have been given." When my husband is away from home, I am the authority in our house, but when he is home, he is the head of our home. You might say, "Well, I am alone because my husband left me for another woman." My question to you is: "Why did you allow him to leave with another woman?" "Why did you allow your husband to leave if you understand that the weapons of your warfare are not of this world?" Some of you might be saying right about now, "But I didn't know how to fight or how to make warfare for that "useless" man who never bothered to take matters into his own hands."

Do you know what Abigail did for her husband Nabal: A shameful drunkard and abuser of women? — Abigail interceded for her husband Nabal when King David wanted to kill him for not feeding his army. Abigail took it upon herself to prepare raisin cakes (1 Samuel 25.18), and much more, and took them to David to prevent him from killing her husband. Abigail found grace with King David who forgave the drunkard's life. Therefore, you are out of excuses! A short time later, Nabal had a heart attack and died. When David heard what happened, he sent for Abigail and took her as his wife — God always rewards our obedience, submission, and respect for authority; whether they deserve it or not.

Remember, vengeance is not yours; it belongs to the Lord. Let God bring you your beloved. If the drunk you used to be married to, died, let God bring you the love of your life; your king. You can be married, single, a virgin, or a young woman; either way, you must begin right now to fight for the high priest of your home to shine. I used to say to the Lord, "I will fight for my husband to shine bright. I recognize that perhaps I have not done my best, but Lord, in what concerns me, I ask for your help to raise the three men that you sent into my life. I may not be the best, but one day, when I come face to face with you, I want to be able to say, 'Lord, you gave me three men, and I did with them what you asked me to do.'" We need to uproot the spirit of indifference from our lives and stop believing that this subject does not concern us. When we finally cast apathy aside, we will see fewer women signing divorce papers and fewer women abandoned by their husbands; we will also see fewer children without fathers.

How many of you today are suffering because the high priest in your home, the authority, is cast down? We can do something about it; something big! We can make the difference. This is the time for us to reflect upon our actions and genuinely repent for resisting the authority. Renew your commitment to pray for the priesthood that was established by God; pray for the people in authority so that we can receive more authority ourselves and be able to come face to face with the authority of God.

CHAPTER VI

COMMITMENT, DISCIPLINE AND PERSEVERANCE

Commitment, discipline, and perseverance are essential virtues that every believer, leader, elder, and minister needs to win spiritual battles; these ingredients make it possible for us to obtain the victory in any war. If we are not totally and completely committed, first with God, and then with our desired objective, we will never lead a disciplined life of constant prayer and perseverance and never reach our desired goal. We call ourselves the army of God, but the moment that we are called to commit ourselves to discipline and perseverance we fall shamefully short of that objective. We want everything to be "microwaveable" (done in seconds). Often, we might have to fight wars that take longer than others, but be encouraged in knowing that the victory is ours. The result of faith is for today, not tomorrow. Take the appropriate action and believe that your blessing and petition is already yours; pray and declare what God wants to give you.

What is "Commitment"?

Commitment means to make a quality decision, to hold fast to that decision for a long period of time, and to do it wholeheartedly without looking back.

> *"¹³Brethren, I do not count myself to have apprehended; but one thing I do, forgetting those things which are behind and reaching forward to those things which are ahead, ¹⁴I press toward the goal for the prize of the upward call of God in Christ Jesus." Philippians 3.13, 14*

What is "Discipline?"

Discipline means to render our flesh into submission in order to achieve a goal.

> *"[12]...rejoicing in hope, patient in tribulation, continuing steadfastly in prayer ..." Romans 12.12*

What was Paul's way to discipline himself?

> *"[27]... but I discipline my body and bring it into subjection, lest, when I have preached to others, I myself should become disqualified."*
> *I Corinthians 9.27*

What is "Perseverance?"

Perseverance means to insist; to remain steady and constant with a person or a thing.

> *"[14]These all continued with one accord in prayer and supplication, with the women and Mary the mother of Jesus, and with His brothers." Acts 1.14*

We must commit ourselves with our Heavenly Father because He seeks people who will adore him in Spirit and in truth. As for me, I decided to meet the Lord at a specific hour every morning, rain or shine; there are no valid excuses to not meet with Him — I will keep my word to God. That is why I wake up at the same time every morning, regardless of what time I go to bed, whether it is early or late, whether I am tired or in pain. I never allow anything to stop me; there is no excuse that is acceptable or reasonable that can keep me away from the Lord; I do not listen to my flesh — our commitment to our Lord is how we demonstrate our love for Jesus. We must be radical children of God and not allow the pebbles in our spiritual walk to keep us away or to stop us from meeting our beloved Jesus of Nazareth at the appointed time. I decided to spend quality time with Him during the early hours of the morning, while everyone else sleeps and before the worries of the day begin. If we do not seek Jesus during the early hours of the morning, we run the risk of beginning the day and leaving home without God's protection. We need to spend time with Him in order to win the battles that await us each day.

We have asked the people who used to practice Satanism the following question: "Whom does the devil attack most?" the answer was always the same; the devil attacks the weaker Christians because they do not pray, read the Word, and they never receive revelation or impartation from God. The devil attacks the people who still have doors open to their spiritual life and who still befriend the world; those who never or rarely attend church. These people become the devil's target; thus, the importance of commitment, discipline, and perseverance in our daily relationship with the Lord so that we can be strengthened to fight the daily battles.

> *"⁷Ask, and it will be given to you; seek, and you will find; knock, and it will be opened to you."*
> *Matthew 7.7*

It is time for the men, the head of their homes, to commit themselves to Jesus. This means that men should be the first to pray, the first to serve, the first to give offerings, the first to praise, and to worship the Lord, so that their wives and children can gladly follow them; together, they will cause the glory of God and His blessings to descend into their homes.

Right now, I encourage you to declare the following prayer together with me. This prayer will encourage you to jump-start your spiritual life once more. After you finish praying with me, make a corresponding action that goes in line with your faith, and begin to live the most beautiful experience of your life which is talking to God and learning to hear His voice to receive direction and blessings for your life.

"Father, in the name of Jesus of Nazareth, I ask that every person reading this book right now: every man, woman, young adult, elderly person, or child, receive the impartation of the Holy Spirit. May they renew their commitment with You to pray everyday because they have understood, through the testimony of our ministry, that prayer opens the door for You to act on their behalf. May they understand that prayer is the only method that establishes your Kingdom and your will in their lives; in the name of Jesus, Amen."

CHAPTER VII

PRAYER OBSTACLES

God's children are called to deliver the captives in the name of Jesus, to speak the Word of God, and to sow love and hope in the hearts of the brokenhearted and those who were abandoned.

"¹The Spirit of the Lord GOD is upon Me, because the LORD has anointed Me to preach good tidings to the poor; He has sent Me to heal the brokenhearted, to proclaim liberty to the captives, and the opening of the prison to those who are bound; ²to proclaim the acceptable year of the LORD, and the day of vengeance of our God; to comfort all who mourn, ³to console those who mourn in Zion, to give them beauty for ashes, the oil of joy for mourning, the garment of praise for the spirit of heaviness; that they may be called trees of righteousness, the planting of the LORD, that He may be glorified." ⁴And they shall rebuild the old ruins, they shall raise up the former desolations, and they shall repair the ruined cities, the desolations of many generations. ⁵Strangers shall stand and feed your flocks and the sons of the foreigner shall be your plowmen and your vinedressers. ⁶But you shall be named the priests of the LORD, they shall call you the servants of our God. You shall eat the riches of the Gentiles, and in their glory you shall boast. ⁷Instead of your shame you shall have double honor, and instead of confusion they shall rejoice in their portion. Therefore in their land they shall possess double; Everlasting joy shall be theirs. ⁸"For I, the LORD, love justice; I hate robbery for burnt offering; I will

direct their work in truth, and will make with them an everlasting covenant. ⁹Their descendants shall be known among the Gentiles and their offspring among the people. All who see them shall acknowledge them, that they are the posterity whom the LORD has blessed." ¹⁰I will greatly rejoice in the LORD, my soul shall be joyful in my God; For He has clothed me with the garments of salvation, He has covered me with the robe of righteousness, as a bridegroom decks himself with ornaments, and as a bride adorns herself with her jewels. ¹¹For as the earth brings forth its bud, as the garden causes the things that are sown in it to spring forth, so the Lord GOD will cause righteousness and praise to spring forth before all the nations." Isaiah 61.1-11

When Christians receive the revelation and conviction that they have authority in the name of Jesus and when they learn to rebuke the legal rights that the enemy has against them, they will become powerful weapons for the Kingdom of God. This authority empowers us to stand firm before the enemy and any other obstacle. With this power we can say: "By the hand of God I cast out demons." To be able to exercise this authority, it is necessary for God's children to stop bickering and complaining and to stop lending their mouths to the devil which he will use to speak his lies. When a Christian stands in authority and makes the Word of God his own, as stated in Jeremiah 1.4-10, then he will begin to see his prayers answered.

"⁴Then the word of the LORD came to me, saying: ⁵"Before I formed you in the womb I knew you; before you were born I sanctified you; I ordained you a prophet to the nations." ⁶Then said I: "Ah, Lord GOD! Behold, I cannot speak, for I am a youth." ⁷But the LORD said to me: "Do not say, 'I am a youth,' for you shall go to all to whom I send you, and whatever I command you, you shall speak. ⁸Do not be afraid of their faces, for I am with you to deliver you," says the LORD. ⁹Then the LORD put

forth His hand and touched my mouth and the LORD said to me: "Behold, I have put My words in your mouth. ¹⁰See, I have this day set you over the nations and over the kingdoms, to root out and to pull down, to destroy and to throw down, to build and to plant." Jeremiah 1.4-10

If you believe this Word and engrave it into your spirit, it will lead you to the place where you will know, with certainty and conviction, that regardless how small you might think you are God makes you a giant with the ability to destroy, to pull down, and to root out the enemy's plans. We have the Word of God, the anointing of the Holy Spirit of God, the blood, and the powerful name of Jesus available for us to use as our weapons of our warfare. In other words, we have everything within our reach to build up, raise up, and root out. Unfortunately, many of our prayers never enter the throne of grace; why do you think that is?

Have you ever asked yourself why there never seems to be a breakthrough in your prayers? I will answer that question for you. If you present yourself before God with impure intentions and motivations, your prayers will have to overcome many obstacles before they can reach God's presence. Also, if you aproach God in this condition, you will lack authority against the devil because there are areas in your life that still belong to the enemy. The Word of God is powerful to cast down strongholds; it is also a double-edged sword — an effective weapon that you must learn to use.

Every obstacle of prayer must be uprooted and destroyed from your life, from your mind, and from your daily living in order to be promoted from prayer into warfare; to become a victorious soldier and not a casualty of war.

As you read each of the following obstacles, examine yourself to see if any of them are present in your life; if they are, renounce them immediately so that you can win the war and conquer the enemy that is trying to destroy your life and the life of others. If you complain, if you allow frustration to take over your emotions, or if you back down in fear, you will lose everything that you gained. For that reason, confess the positive by declaring God's Word; confess God's promises, the ones that He has for you and your loved ones. If you do this nonstop, then, even when you feel unsteady and shaky, you will complete God's plan for your life.

SIN

One of the most powerful obstacles of prayer is sin. If you have sin in your life and choose not to repent, your prayers are blocked and the enemy gains legal entrance into areas of your life where he will take over and begin to govern. One person cannot be a part of the kingdom of light while behaving and participating as a member of the kingdom of darkness — we are either children of light or children of darkness; therefore, it is necessary for that person to repent immediately and stop the cycle of sin. Now, if you believe that your obstacle seems to be a compulsive behavior that you cannot deal with on your own, then you need to find someone to help you be free. You need another person to break the bondage, the iniquity, and every alliance created with the enemy.

UNFORGIVENESS

Another powerful obstacle in prayer is unforgiveness; it stops our spiritual growth. Unforgiveness is like a deadly spiritual virus that spreads throughout our hearts and minds causing the love and joy in us to deteriorate with hate and bitterness; it destroys us. Forgiveness, on the other hand, is the antidote to the enemy's plan of destruction for our lives. When we choose a lifestyle of forgiveness, our prayers will be effective and they will bring forth fruit. Although it is often excruciatingly difficult to forgive, we should never base our decision to forgive based on how we feel about the person or the situation; we need to forgive because God commands it. When we learn to forgive every time that we suffer an injustice, and when we condition our minds to do it, we eliminate and destroy the devil's right to torment our emotions.

Our refusal to forgive is a subconscious declaration that we think of ourselves as being better than God; He forgave our past, present, and future sin in one moment — the sacrifice of Jesus Christ at the cross. He forgives us continually because He loves us. If we have unresolved issues with our parents and for some reason we have not forgiven them, we should ask ourselves the following question: "Am I better than God to choose not to forgive them?" If we search our hearts and find that there are still unresolved issues of unforgiveness on our part, we need to ask God to forgive us for holding on to resentment. Do you remember what Jesus said to Peter?

> *"21 Then Peter came to Him and said, "Lord, how often shall my brother sin against me, and I forgive him? Up to seven times?" 22 Jesus said to him, "I do not say to you, up to seven times, but up to seventy times seven." Matthew 18.21, 22*

Forgiveness should be a lifestyle choice for us; we must forgive those who have caused us pain; we need to renounce and reject every ounce of contamination and influence that encourages unforgiveness, hate, resentment and bitterness before it destroys us and our relationship with God. Right now, I invite you to let go of the spirit of unforgiveness — begin by breathing deeply, inhale and exhale; while you are doing this, keep in mind that you are letting loose and letting go of every spirit that was lodged in your heart and mind from the moment that the door was opened to unforgiveness. When there is unforgiveness in our hearts, there are also physical symptoms that become obvious when we hear someone speak of the person who hurt us; we might even experience a physical reaction at the mention of their name which will include stomach cramps or chest pains. These symptoms could be indicative that spirits are lodged in our bodies; once we renounce these spirits, we will take back any legal rights that they might have against us. Forgiveness is a crucial step that we must take if we want to see our prayers answered; it is essential if we want to see positive change and to bring forth fruit in any area of our lives. When Jesus enters our hearts, it becomes easy to forgive because the Holy Spirit helps us to do it; not only does He help us to forgive, He also helps us to heal the areas of our lives that were hurting. Believe the revelation of this word — do not just read it and then forget about it, practice forgiveness! Experience God's Word and give testimony to others of what this revelation has done for your life. The glory belongs to our Lord and Savior, Jesus Christ.

MARITAL PROBLEMS

When the husband seeks to do what is right for his wife, or vice versa, many wonderful things can be accomplished. On the other hand, when he or she is only looking out for number one, it can destroy the marital relationship. If we want our prayers to reach the Throne of Grace, we must be in good standing with our spouse; to accomplish this, we need to learn how to communicate effectively. This is not a difficult thing to do when we trust in God and in His gift of love; when we learn to love our spouse unconditionally — in the same way that God loves us — we will also learn to forgive and to pray for them. When we fight with our spouse, we lose the battle against the enemy and we miss out on the victory that should have been ours in the Lord.

Women should, and must, submit to the authority and love of their husbands. Although we might be right, we should stay quiet. I understand that keeping quiet is not always easy, but do not become discouraged because we are not losers when we keep our mouths shut with our spouse and vent with the Lord.

I love to submit to authority and I am sure that I learned to do it by watching how my mother obeyed and respected my father's authority; although she was known as "the lioness" because of her strong character and personality, the person who wore the "pants" (authority) and the last word at home was my father. For every man who reads this book, please know that if you submit to Christ, who is the head of every man, you will automatically become the head of your home. When you submit to Christ, you will be a good leader in the home and your wife will have no trouble submitting to your love and gentle guidance. However, when these conditions are not in place, the divine order of authority that was established by God is broken and the family suffers the consecuences. Therefore, it is neces- sary for you, as the high priest of your home, to rise to the occa- sion and submit to Christ; fasting and praying will empower you to become a true spiritual leader and a good role model to your wife and children.

Ladies, if your spouse is not a man given to prayer, do not fight him or force him to do it. Instead, to encourage him, begin to pray; this will make your husband feel uncomfortable for not doing it. If you continue to believe in the power of prayer, the moment will come when your husband will take his role as head and leader. Your husband will assume his true role as high priest in the home, and you will become the ideal helper (the one who surrounds and protects her husband with prayer). Each spouse must fight his/her own battle without fighting or having discus- sions with the spouse; it can easily be accomplished by doing what is right before God — keep quiet and pray! Do not fight with your spouse; instead, fight against Satan. Hold your place on the offensive side and fight the devil everyday; force him to retreat and to loosen your spouse!

When a couple prays together, they form a powerful attack team that is capable of penetrating the devil's defense; together, they can rescue their children, their families, and their neighbors from the devil's grip.

If you do not see immediate results, do not give up; keep fight- ing the devil and keep praying because sooner or later you will see results.

DISOBEDIENCE TO GOD'S WORD

> *"⁹One who turns away his ear from hearing the law, even his prayer is an abomination."*
> Proverbs 28.9

We must make the decision to say "NO" to the world and to the desires of the flesh. God has the same blessings for everyone, but it depends on us if we are to receive them or not. Our level of spiritual growth depends entirely on us — the person who closes his ears to avoid hearing the law should not expect to have his prayers heard.

If we have chosen not to hear the Word of God and to disobey what it says, we ought to repent right now and ask God for a new beginning; there is always hope in Christ because "His mercies are new every day."

It is an incredible blessing to serve God, but for us to serve Him, it is necessary to let go of malice and sin. Not obeying God's Word is an obstacle to our prayers; it is also a negative testimony and lifestyle. If the Lord is asking us to separate ourselves from sin, and we choose not to obey, then our prayers will not be answered and we will have to suffer the consequences of our actions. We must learn to hear God's Word; we must learn it, practice it, and obey it in order to receive blessings until they "runneth over".

PRAYING FOR THE WRONG THINGS

Our prayers are fruitless when we:

• Do not spend time in prayer for others.
• Are selfish in the way we pray.
• Make prayers of manipulation through which we want our will to be done and not His.
• Pray for our own benefit.

We must have the right motivation when we ask God for anything and it must be the something that gives Him the glory and the honor. When we ask with selfish reasons, we waste our time because God is not going to honor our prayers.

Now that you understand the importance of prayer and its obstacles, and now that you know that the prayer of the righteous is effective, you must choose to tear down, pull down, and root out that which is preventing your prayers from being effective and pleasing unto God. Now is the time to live like a true Christian; praying constantly so that God can show you the areas of your life that you must change, thus making it possible for Him to use you. If you want to be used by God, and if you want to pass from **prayer into warfare** and become a powerful weapon in the Lord's army, you must remove every obstacle that stands in your way and dedicate your life, and every area of it, to God. Surrender your weaknesses to the Lord; the Heavenly Father will never reject a humble and contrite heart.

CHAPTER VIII

INTERCESSION

If we believe that we are incapable of doing warfare it is because, in our own eyes, we see ourselves as weak and powerless to change the circumstances or situations that arise; we enter the battlefield and prepare to fight in our own strength, but wars are fought in God's strength not ours. In Him, we are always winners!

Eliminate that mentality that says "I can't" and present yourself before your Heavenly Father as a bondservant and a child of God. We have the authority, in the name of Jesus, to take back the people and nations that up until now have been under the devil's grip. It is necessary to eliminate self-pity from our lives and allow God to use us and to pour His new wine in us.

God is not looking for people with titles; He is looking for people with willing hearts. The only thing that we need is faith and boldness to believe that whatever God asks, it will be done in the name of Jesus and in the power of His blood.

Take His cross and follow Him. Do not worry about what others might say about you and do not fret over how much pain they caused. Set aside your past and follow Jesus; keep your eyes on Him and not on the people around you. Begin to pray because the Lord is seeking men and women who are willing to raise a hedge of protection for His people.

> *"[12]And from the days of John the Baptist until now the kingdom of heaven suffers violence and the violent take it by force." Matthew 11.12*

It is necessary to crave the manifestation of the kingdom of God with great passion, desire, and effort. To accomplish this, you must pay the price. You must stop complaining and stop inviting yourself to pity-parties. Decide today to stand up in the powerful name of Jesus!

When my husband and I started in ministry, we were heavily attacked by the enemy. However, the Holy Spirit taught me to make warfare against the enemy and to stand in the gap for my family. I did everything that the Lord instructed me to do. I said, "Devil, this is as far as you can come, do not dare touch my home or my ministry because my older brother, Jesus of Nazareth, the One who defeated you on the cross of Calvary and took back the keys of hell and death from you, is holding my hand right now. If you dare come against me, you are going to be dealing with Him, not me." The devil hates to hear that. When he attacks you with lies such as, "You can't" or if he tries to destroy your home, your ministry, or your children, knock him down and send him flying with the Word of God; remind him of his future. This is war!

You make war when you are an intercessor, when you are a repairer of bridges and gaps for your husband, your children, and your entire family. Ask the Holy Spirit to give you strategies on how to protect your loved ones. To accomplish this, you must learn to raise the hedge of protection, the fortress, so that when the enemy comes he will not have access to your family.

God is seeking true worshippers and intercessors. Think about this: if He is "looking" for them, it must mean that there are only a few worshippers and intercessors. Remember, God decided to use our bodies to accomplish His plans on earth. Therefore, prepare yourself so that He can use your body, your mouth, your hands, and all that you are.

> "[24]God is Spirit, and those who worship Him must worship in spirit and truth." John 4.24

To become intercessors or repairers of the gap, it is necessary to be a true worshipper and to love God with all your hearts (in body, soul, and spirit). Also, you must seek Him and tell Him that you want Him to do whatever He sees fit; whatever He wants to do with you, for His honor and glory.

Intercession raises a hedge of protection; a fortress that helps those who are in difficult situations. Intercession protects those who feel desperate, and it is a fortified wall that is raised with God's Word when it is declared and decreed over people, ministries, families, or nations. The individual who prays and intercedes believes that God can use him to accomplish a lot more than just asking for himself.

When the family, a spouse, a ministry, or a nation are covered with prayer, it means that a fortified wall has been raised with the Word of God which the enemy cannot penetrate regardless of how hard he tries; this wall is a protective barrier that keeps them safe. You could be the builder of that fortified wall that protects your loved ones if you dare to believe it and if you are ready to win the war through prayer. You must build the hedge of protection with the Word of God, the name of Jesus, and the power of the blood of the Lamb. You have the Lord's arsenal at your disposal; there you will find the weapons of your warfare which are not carnal but powerful in God. If the center of your life is the King of kings and the Lord of lords — Jesus of Nazareth — if your foundation includes prayer and if you are a willing vessel, then go ahead and say: "Lord, I place my spiritual womb at your disposal so that through prayer I can birth the salvation of my family, my neighbors, and the nation." By using your mouth, you will accomplish great things in the name of Jesus.

Go to the next level where you will be able to penetrate the defenses of the enemy; the level where the anointing to destroy, pull down, root out, and destroy every work of the devil is received. Rise to the level where you can begin to plant the Word of God; where you must be as God's child. This is the level that goes beyond prayer and into war.

A couple of years ago during a prayer vigil, I interceded for my father until I birthed him in the spirit. In the name of Jesus, I destroyed the plans of the enemy against him, and I planted the Word in his life. A short time later, I received a phone call urging me to travel to Colombia to say my good-byes because the doctors had said that my father only had a short time to live. When I arrived in Colombia, I talked to him about Jesus of Nazareth, and I shared with him everything that Jesus had done in my life; I told him that I was thankful to God for the father that He had given me. I started to thank my father for being a good role model in my life and for the simple fact that he was my father. Also, I told him that he was the best father in the world and that his life had made an impact on mine because he had been an excellent father. Suddenly, my father started to cry out; he screamed and cried. I realized then that what was killing him was the spirit of guilt. For God's glory and honor, my father was healed that day. More than five years have come and gone since that day at the hospital and my father is still healthy and rejuvenated. After he left the hospital, he started to preach to his neighbors and today he is a powerful Christian leader. He is a man who fasts and prays and he is an incredible worshipper. When we surrender to God and when we allow the Holy Spirit to take over our lives and use us, He can do anything through us.

Surrender your life to God. Give Him your mouth and speak His words. Repair the bridges and stand in the gap; build fortified walls and watch how God will glorify His name through you.

CHAPTER IX

POSSESSING THE KEYS TO THE KINGDOM

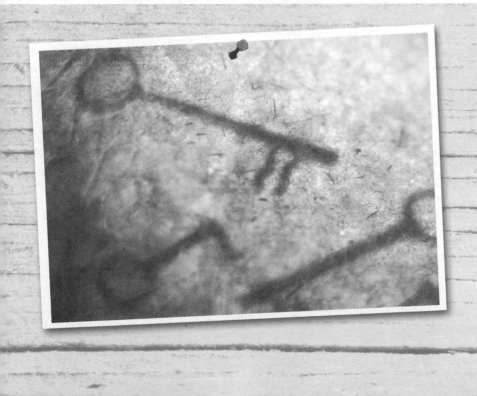

One important thing that must be understood by believers is that each of us has received power and authority to represent God, to execute dominion, and to exercise our lordship on earth. God created man to have lordship over all created things. Therefore, everything that we allow to happen or loosen on earth is allowed in heaven, and everything that we bind on earth is bound in heaven.

God created man to have lordship over all created things

> "²⁶Then God said, "Let Us make man in Our image, according to Our likeness; let them have dominion over the fish of the sea, over the birds of the air, and over the cattle, over all the earth and over every creeping thing that creeps on the earth.""
> Genesis 1.26

When God tells man to exert dominion over all created things, He is saying to exert dominion, lordship, authority, and to execute or complete His designs and plans. He gave man legal rights to fulfill His plans and purpose on earth.

How was man going to establish his lordship?

From the beginning, God established in His Word that to execute authority on earth, it would be necessary to have a physical body. Otherwise, a being that operates on earth without a physical body would be operating illegally.

God gives man the authority to exercise his lordship on earth in the following two ways:

Through a physical body. The physical body gives man rights to live on earth legally and to exercise dominion and lordship over all created things; thus, fulfilling God's plans for humanity.

Through our free will. From the beginning, God established in His Word that He gave man free will to choose and to make his own decisions. God has never violated a person's free will. Therefore, for man to exercise his lordship on earth he must make himself available to God, and of his own free will, he must tell God: "Yes sir, I will obey with joy and happiness." He must offer his body to God so that He can dwell within man's heart and complete His purpose on earth.

Man's downfall into sin

Adam did not exercise his lordship and authority over his wife or over the snake. Notice that the devil used the serpent's body to tempt Eve because he clearly understood God's biblical principal which states that before one can take any action on earth, one must have a body. Therefore, Adam and Eve fall to temptation and sin; they lose their authority and the power given to them by God. As a consequence, now man finds himself in need of redemption from sin.

Jesus takes back the authority that was once lost

Jesus came to earth. He was born of a virgin. He came to earth as a man in a physical body which granted Him the legal right to act and to move on earth. Jesus suffers on the cross, and on the third day, He is raised from the dead thereby taking back, through His death, the authority and the power that was once lost in order to turn it over to the church. In simpler terms, He gave us, the believers, the authority and power that were lost in the Garden.

> "*[18]And Jesus came and spoke to them, saying, "All authority has been given to Me in heaven and on earth." Matthew 28.18*

The word **authority** is found in every Biblical translation. Every time we see the word **authority** it refers to the power, right, ability, and influence that were given to every believer by our Lord Jesus to exercise dominion and lordship over all things on earth. Jesus took back what Adam had lost and turned it over to us, the church.

What is authority?

In Greek, the word *"exousia"* means the delegated legal rights to exercise dominion and lordship with a power that backs it up. The word "power" is often used in the legal field. In this chapter, we will learn the meaning of this word.

What is power?

Power is the authority, the capability, or ability to accomplish any task with legal rights granted by the other party.

What is a power of attorney?

A power of attorney is a legal document written by one person, the principal party, which grants legal rights to another person to exercise certain and specific acts and tasks in the absence of or in the name of the principal party. This power of attorney is also enforced in the event of death of the principal party, in which case the receiving agent automatically receives the full delegated power to act on behalf of the deceased.

> *"16...for where there is a testament, there must also of necessity be the death of the testator. 17For a testament is in force after men are dead, since it has no power at all while the testator lives."*
> Hebrews 9.16, 17

How can we apply this legal act to the spiritual act of Jesus?

Jesus came to earth as a man; he died, and on the third day, He was raised from the dead. His resurrection granted the church legal rights which were left to us in writing. In this document, the principal party is the Lord of heaven and earth, and we, the church, are His authorized agents. God entrusted us with His authority to complete or to exercise His will on His behalf. We, the believers, have "written legal rights" to prohibit or to allow, to open or to close, to cast out demons and to heal the sick, to pray and to intercede for any thing on earth. Praise God!

There are two types of "legal powers" in modern law:

A specific power. This power is given to act only in specific cases or occurrences on behalf of the principal party.

A general power. This power is granted, thus giving legal rights to act and to exercise in any situation on behalf of the principal party. In this type of power, the principal party gives and bestows every right to the agent to represent him and to act on his behalf, not only in the area of decision making, but also when it comes to doing whatever is necessary to accomplish that which was entrusted to the agent to do through the power of attorney and which was granted by the principal party.

Jesus did not give us a specific power but rather a general power of attorney to exercise and to complete everything that He has entrusted for us to do.

When Jesus said these words: *"And Jesus came and spoke to them, saying, 'All authority has been given to Me in heaven and on earth. Go therefore...'"* He was placing in our hands a blank check or a general power. In other words, Jesus was giving us the same authority that was granted to Him by the Heavenly Father. Praise God!

Jesus delegates this "general legal power" to us so that we could cast out demons.

> *"[18]And He said to them, "I saw Satan fall like lightning from heaven. [19]Behold, I give you the authority*

> *to trample on serpents and scorpions, and over all the power of the enemy, and nothing shall by any means hurt you." Luke 10.18, 19*

The word **trample** in Greek is the word *"pateo"* which means to pound, crush, mash, bruise, and step on, or to stand on with one's foot.

Jesus gave us the general power of attorney to step on every wicked work of the devil. He said: *"I give you the authority to trample, to pound, crush, mash, bruise, step on, and stand on serpents, scorpions, and over all the power of the enemy."* We, the believers, are called to take action in the name of Jesus, at all times and in any circumstance, and to confront the devil and his demons.

The legal rights or general power given by Jesus is backed by a heavenly power. Not only did Jesus leave this power of attorney in writing, He also wants us to exercise it; He gave us the power to use it. An example of this entrusted power can be seen when the President of the United States establishes a decree, not only verbally, but also in writing. This decree is a law that must be respected and obeyed. If any citizen chooses not to obey his decree, the President has under his command the entire armed forces: the Air Force, the Marines, the Army, the Navy, and the Judges, Congress, the Senate, the FBI, and CIA that stand by him ready to enforce his decree and laws.

If citizens choose not to submit to the law, then one or many governmental branches will make sure that these rebellious and disobedient individuals obey. If they still refuse to obey, then they will be incarcerated.

The President has so much support that any time he commands anything to be done, it is immediately done. The same thing occurs in the spiritual realm. Jesus entrusted us with a power of attorney to execute everything that He left in writing for us to do.

Furthermore, if someone does not want to submit to the laws of the kingdom, we have the power that was entrusted to us by Jesus to make certain that whatever must be done is completed. We have His name, the Word of God, the anointing of the Holy Spirit, the precious blood of Jesus, the angels of heaven, and a power that endorses, supports, and backs up what we do on earth.

The power that supports us to execute the authority that we have on earth is received when the Holy Spirit comes upon us and we are filled with His presence. The evidence that this power has come upon us is the speaking in other tongues.

> *"⁸...but you shall receive power when the Holy Spirit has come upon you; and you shall be witnesses to Me in Jerusalem, and in all Judea and Samaria, and to the end of the earth.""* Acts 1.8

What is included in the power of attorney that was left to us by Jesus in writing?

> *"¹⁹And I will give you the keys of the kingdom of heaven, and whatever you bind on earth will be bound in heaven, and whatever you loose on earth will be loosed in heaven.""* Matthew 16.19

What is the meaning of the word "bind"?

The word **bind** in Greek is the word *"deo"* which means to attach, connect, join, combine, unite, tie, fasten, restrict, arrest, prohibit, and to declare something illegal or illegitimate and improper.

Another meaning to the word "bind" in Greek is *"deesis"* which is translated as prayer or supplication. In other words, "to bind" is an action that is attached or connected to intercession. Therefore, we have the authority to bind through the act of intercession.

What is the meaning of the word "loosen"?

The word "**loosen**" in Greek is the word "**luo**" which means to untie, unbind, undue, release, or to allow; to grant permission to operate, to declare something legal or legitimate, to declare something proper, or to open or to remove.

When Jesus tells Peter, *"Whatever you bind on earth will be bound in heaven,"* he is really saying:

"I, as the Lord of heaven and earth, am giving you a written will where I appoint or assign you to be my ambassadors, my agents, my children, and my representatives on earth. You have a physical body that gives you legal rights to live and to operate on earth. Now, I also entrust you with authority, potential, and legal rights. I bestow upon you the power of attorney to bind, to restrict, to close, and to prohibit; to declare improper and illegal everything that must be restricted on earth. This shall also be done as you say in heaven. Everything that you bind, close, tie, and restrict on earth will also be closed, tied, and restricted in heaven." Jesus tells us to exercise our authority because we have the right to do it. In other words, He is making us responsible for everything that happens on earth. Jesus also said, "And whatever you loosen on earth will be loosened in heaven."

If we are experiencing demonic oppression, it is because we have not taken authority over it; we have allowed the devil to come against us. If our home is in ruins, it is our responsibility because we have allowed the devil to come against us while we did nothing to stop him. If the enemy has caused our bodies to be sick, then we neglected to prohibit the devil to touch our bodies. If any doors of curse or damnation, depression, or misery are opened, it is because we have not exercised our authority to close them. If the enemy has caused quarreling and division in our families, it is because we have not declared his presence and wrongful doings in our homes illegal; we have not ordered him to leave. If the door of a better employment opportunity has not opened, then we have not exercised our authority to open that door.

It is a powerful, impressive, and wonderful thing to understand everything that the Lord has provided His church. He makes us powerful and enables us to operate with the authority to bind and loosen, to prohibit or to allow, to open or to close anything on earth.

The moment that Jesus gave us this authority, He made us responsible for our actions and decisions and for everything that happens around us. Jesus is no longer responsible for our actions because He provided everything that we need to declare the victory.

No longer can we cast blame on anyone for our poor living conditions. Whatever happens to us is the direct result of our neglect to prohibit or to declare it illegal in our lives. Our lack of action allows things to happen in our lives.

How do we bind and loosen?

We bind and loosen through intercession

Intercession is the path that we must use to close and to open, to prohibit or to allow, to bind the devil and to loosen someone that is oppressed or enslaved by the enemy. Through intercession, we, the believers, can forbid the enemy to inflict our families with sickness. We can open ministerial doors or employment opportunities that were closed or beyond our reach. We can deliver the captives and set them free and we can declare illegal and improper every work of witchcraft, sorcery, argumentation, dissension, and opposition. Our intercession has the power to change everything around us. God cannot resist the devil for us. It is up to us to resist the devil.

> *"⁷Therefore submit to God. Resist the devil and he will flee from you." James 4.7*

We bind and loosen through revelation

> *"¹⁷Jesus answered and said to him, "Blessed are you, Simon Bar-Jonah, for flesh and blood has not revealed this to you, but My Father who is in heaven." Matthew 16.17*

What is "revelation"?

The word "**revelation**" is *"Apocalipsis"* in Greek; it means to expose, to disclose, or to reveal a hidden truth.

A revelation is an action used by God to communicate or to disclose into our spirit and mind an unknown truth. This truth is not something that suddenly came into existence but a truth found in the Bible that had been overlooked, misunderstood, or never seen.

The revelation or understanding concerning something in particular is the key that we need to intercede and to exercise the power to bind and to loosen. If we lack revelation and understanding in a certain area, we will not be able to exercise our authority appropriately. Remember, Jesus left us a written will that we must read, know, and obtain revelation from. In the Constitution of the United States, we find a writing that says, "Ignorance of the law is not an excuse."

It is our responsibility to seek, research, and investigate; to inquire into, and to understand what is written in the will left to us by Jesus. We need to search the Word to understand our rights, privileges, and responsibilities before we can exercise our authority to bind and to loosen.

The strongest weapon that the enemy has used for many centuries to paralyze the believer from exercising his authority is the weapon of ignorance. Although many believers have, in theory, the legal power or the power of attorney to exercise their dominion and lordship in Jesus' name, they cannot enforce it because of their ignorance and because they do not have or understand the revelation of the Word.

Who holds the keys of the kingdom?

The keys of the kingdom are in the hands of believers who receive the revelation of the Word. Some individuals have tried to exercise their authority and the results have been shameful because of their lack of revelation and understanding in what they were doing.

> *"13Then some of the itinerant Jewish exorcists took it upon themselves to call the name of the Lord Jesus over those who had evil spirits, saying, "We exorcise you by the Jesus whom Paul preaches!" Acts 19.13*

Every time that God reveals a truth unknown to us or a truth that we do not understand, He is placing in our hands a key to open a door in the Spirit.

A key represents the revelation of a Biblical truth.

The kingdom of God is like a great mansion with a million rooms. To open each door, and to enter any room, a key is needed, and this key is the revelation of the Word in a specific area. How can we apply this truth to our lives? The moment that God reveals a truth of the Word in the area of inner healing and deliverance, intercession, prosperity, authority, power, holiness, or any other Biblical truth, He is placing a key in our hands that unlocks the treasures found behind that door or area. This is why the enemy wants to keep us in the dark about such things. Because when the believer learns to intercede with revelation and understanding concerning that which he is praying and believing for, and when he exercises his authority over it, his prayers and intercession become effective as he prohibits, binds, and declares illegal and improper that which is wicked.

Why did Jesus give Peter the keys?

> *"19And I will give you the keys of the kingdom of heaven, and whatever you bind on earth will be*

bound in heaven, and whatever you loose on earth will be loosed in heaven." Matthew 16.19

Jesus gave Peter the keys to the kingdom at that moment because he received the revelation directly from God. The same thing happens when we receive a revelation.

Many Believers do not Receive the Revelation from God

Although it is God's desire to give us revelation and understanding of His Word, not everyone is willing, able, or prepared to receive new truths. God does not allow certain things to be revealed to all people.

In the four gospels, Jesus spoke in parables to His disciples. When they asked Him why, Jesus answered and said that it was to hide the revelation and truth of that word from those who did not earnestly want it. Jesus opens the eyes of their understanding to those who hunger and thirst for the Word of God.

> *"¹¹He answered and said to them, "Because it has been given to you to know the mysteries of the kingdom of heaven, but to them it has not been given..." Matthew 13.11*

God does not reveal His mysteries to the whole world. He reveals them to those who truly desire, with all their heart, to know more of Him.

God's judgment against prideful and arrogant people is spiritual blindness. It is very difficult, almost an impossibility, for a proud believer to receive a revelation from God. One way that God hides His truths from arrogant people is to blind the eyes of their understanding so that they will not exalt themselves and to prevent them from trusting in their own wisdom.

Who receives the revelation from God?

> *"²¹In that hour Jesus rejoiced in the Spirit and said, "I thank You, Father, Lord of heaven and earth, that You have hidden these things from the wise and prudent and revealed them to babes. Even so, Father, for so it seemed good in Your sight."*
> *Luke 10.21*

In this verse, the word "**babes**" is not referring to children, those who are young in age, but it represents the mind and heart of a child. A child is teachable — someone who is not yet specialized or trained. A child lacks expertise; he is humble and meek.

Jesus is trying to teach us that revelation is received by believers who are "like" children; who have a teachable heart. The revelation is received by believers who do not consider themselves experts and who are continuously learning; believers who do not trust in the knowledge presented by the world, but those who are humble and gentle. These are the ones who receive the revelation, and because of it, they have the power to bind and loosen, to prohibit and to allow, to open and to close.

If you are a believer who thinks of yourself as wise, you will never walk in the revelation of the Word or in the knowledge of God. You will live in darkness and obscurity. Where there is ignorance, there is darkness.

Many teaching institutions teach theology, but people are honestly tired of so much "information". People want revelation that produces change.

What causes the revelation of the Word in a believer?

CHANGES IN THE PERSON AND HIS DESTINY.

> *"¹⁷Jesus answered and said to him, "Blessed are you, Simon Bar-Jonah, for flesh and blood has not revealed this to you, but My Father who is in heaven." Matthew 16.17*

The name "Simon" means a weak reed (any of various tall grasses that grow especially in wet areas; a person or thing too weak to rely on; one easily swayed or overcome). Therefore, the name "Simon" represents or symbolizes a believer without revelation of the Word.

It represents a believer who is emotionally unstable, weak and who is easily swayed or overcome. It also means one who is easily defeated in any circumstance; one who is easily discouraged or depressed.

Now, let us read what happened to Simon after receiving the revelation that Jesus was the Messiah.

> *"18And I also say to you that you are Peter, and on this rock I will build My church, and the gates of Hades shall not prevail against it." Matthew 16.18*

The name "Peter" in Greek is the word **"petros"** which means a stone, a rock, a ledge, or cliff. Peter is symbolic of a mature believer; one who is stable, solid, and a living rock.

> *"5...you also, as living stones, are being built up a spiritual house, a holy priesthood, to offer up spiritual sacrifices acceptable to God through Jesus Christ." 1 Peter 2.5*

Peter represents a believer who is emotionally stable, mature, and able to withstand the pressures of ministry and service to God and the oppression of the enemy. **"Petros"** is a solid rock that holds up and strengthens others; one who has the revelation of the authority to bind and loosen.

The revelation of God's Word changes the nature and destiny of a person. This means that if we used to be carnal believers (Simon), easily swayed, emotionally unstable and immature, when we receive the revelation, we change and become mature believers (Peter), stable, solid, and able to intercede with the revelation; thus, making our prayers more effective.

When God's revelation enters our hearts, it touches us deeply, with such conviction, that it causes us to act; it turns us into a firm rock.

THE REVELATION OF THE WORD MAKES US WARRIORS.

> *"[18]And I also say to you that you are Peter, and on this rock I will build My church, and the gates of Hades shall not prevail against it." Matthew 16.18*

> *"[18]And I tell you, you are Peter [Greek, Petros—a large piece of rock], and on this rock [Greek, Petra—a huge rock like Gibraltar] I will build My church, and the gates of Hades (the powers of the infernal region) shall not overpower it [or be strong to its detriment or hold out against it]." Amplified Bible*

The best position we can assume against the enemy is the position of warfare. We attack when we become true warriors.

If we were to draw a conclusion on everything that was covered in this chapter, we would say that God has given us the power of attorney. God has granted us legal rights, the authority, the ability to exercise the written will left to us by Jesus. He left us this authority and made us responsible on earth to make sure that everything runs smoothly. God is not going to resist the enemy for us.

Every believer must resist the devil on his own, and the best weapon available to us to stand against him is intercession. In prayer, we have the authority to open or close, to declare something illegitimate or illegal, but there is a key needed to accomplish this successfully. We need the revelation of what we are praying for. Otherwise, we will not obtain the desired results. It is essential that we receive the revelation, not only to pray effectively, but also to reach the level of a mature and stable believer in the Lord.

CHAPTER X

TESTIMONIES OF RESTORATION

Frank Hechavarria:

My parents were divorced when I was a child, and by the time I turned 11 years old, I had already experienced depression, loneliness, anguish, and the desire to die. In truth, I did not know why I was alive. It is hard to understand such things at any age, but for a child, these were very confusing and troublesome. It was also at the age of 11 that I had my first encounter with Jesus. I remember that one day, while we still lived in Cuba, someone invited my mother to a Christian church; she accepted the invitation and took me along for the ride where we continued to attend the worship services regularly. I was not as committed as I should have been and a short time later I walked away from the Lord straight into the world. In other words, I lived in shameful drunkenness, fornication, and sin, but deep down inside I knew that my lifestyle was wrong. We moved to the United States where I lived life for the moment but something that seemed stronger than me kept urging me to return to church and to the Lord. Five years ago, this silent but powerful urging led my mother and me back to church. We started to attend El Rey Jesus Church where our lives were drastically changed; today, I continue to follow my Lord faithfully. I was 18 when I came to this church — the perfect age for the world to entice me — but thanks to prayer, I learned to have intimacy with the Lord who watched over me and separated me for Him.

Today, I am an addict to prayer! It is the only addiction that does not cause any harm. Through prayer, the Lord has equipped me to overcome the continuous battles that I have to deal with in my flesh each day. I started to pray four years ago from three thirty in the morning till six. I learned that the early morning prayer is powerful. I used to be a man who was easily led to anger. I was like a match, ready to fire up; I would explode over the smallest thing. Anger is an evil that can destroy in one moment what takes years to build; things such as marriages, careers, and ministries. Why pray in the morning instead of at night? — Because at night, you go to sleep without the worries of the new day and its new battles. If you pray only at night, and not in the morning, you walk out of your house unprepared; you walk straight into the traps that the enemy laid out for you and which you will surely run into throughout the day. If you pray in the morning, you are more prepared for that day's journey. Now that I have surrendered the area of anger to the Lord, in prayer, I feel confident and prepared to overcome the temptation of getting angry if it dares to show up. Besides anger, I was able to overcome rejection, loneliness, low self-esteem, and timidity (I used to be an introvert, afraid and incapable of approaching anyone and inept at having a civilized conversation), but the Lord, through prayer, equipped me with His spiritual weapons and now I can definitely declare that I have gone from prayer into warfare. I am a living testimony of the power of prayer. I say this for the glory of God!

Because of what I have gone through, my advice to every person who is experiencing similar problems to mine, or who has had a hard time dealing with lies or difficulty in any other area of their lives, is to surrender these things to the Lord, every day, first thing in the morning, so that God can change them.

Based on my experience, I understand what it is like to walk away from the Lord and also to return. That is why I can assure you that the only thing we need to walk away from the Lord is to stop praying. I am now 24 years old and I am a youth pastor. This privilege would never have been bestowed to me if I were not a man of prayer. Before I knew that my calling was to be a pastor, there was always the deep and heartfelt desire to please God but I was unable to do it in my own strength; I would not be what I am today without God's mercy and prayer. I am eternally thankful to God for everything that He has done in my life and to my pastors for teaching me the importance of prayer in order to establish a true relationship with the Lord. A Christian who does not pray is very close to becoming a non-Christian. Without prayer, people dry up inside and end up being controlled by their own flesh and not by the Spirit.

The early morning prayer teaches us to be thankful and to develop our faith because before the day begins we are already thanking God for what He is about to do that day. Also, prayer sharpens our spiritual ears to clearly hear the voice of God and His plans; this helps us to deal with and overcome the temptations we will face each day and it keeps us from feeling intimidated by the events of the day. Prayer also heals and transforms minds and hearts. Prayer changes the areas that we are unable to change on our own.

A man who does not pray is vulnerable to the constant attacks of the enemy, and he is incapable of accomplishing God's will. Without prayer, men take the risk of losing their blessings and even the call on their lives. Furthermore, they are dominated by the old self. However, the man who keeps himself connected to the Lord through prayer becomes the high priest in his home. He is the first to love, to give offerings, to pray, and he is capable of being a good role model and father.

Every day that we wake up, the enemy is on the prowl seeking to destroy and to devour us; he is constantly designing plans of destruction against us. This is why we must penetrate his territory through prayer, intercession, and spiritual warfare because the violent take the Kingdom of Heaven by force.

Practicing the early morning prayer makes us warriors. I learned this from Pastor Ana Maldonado. This became a reality in my life when I decided to attend the early prayer meetings at church; it was then that I received the spirit of a warrior. She taught me to hate sin, including the sin of independence from God, in order to pass from prayer into warfare.

I invite every person who has been unable to maintain a lifestyle of prayer to read this book. It will lead us to totally surrender our lives and to increase our desire to know God. Once you decide to pray at least ten or fifteen minutes a day, the Lord will begin to require more of you, and in turn, you will want to spend more time with Him. But, it is important to pray everyday; to be constant and faithful. It is worthless to pray one or two days and then not pray again the rest of the week. An unstable prayer life is unacceptable if you want to experience true intimacy with the Lord.

I know that this book will be a great blessing to every one who reads it. From each page in this book, you will be able to take from Pastor Maldonado's spirit and receive the impartation directly from her, which she has acquired throughout the many years in ministry, prayer, spiritual warfare, and by living a life in sanctity and integrity. The anointing for war that resides in Pastors Guillermo and Ana Maldonado, that which is impregnated in each paragraph and testimony found in this book, will lead you from prayer into war, if you make it your own. You will never be the same again; of this, I am certain.

"There is no battle that cannot be won through prayer"

Andy Arguez

My father left me when I was only six years old; his absence affected me greatly. At a very early age, I got involved in drugs, gangs, shoot-outs, drunkenness, fights, and near-death experiences; on more than one occasion, I saw bullets fly close to my face. I confronted death at close range — it is heartbreaking to remember the friends that died over a five dollar bag of marihuana; it is painful to know that many of the people that used to be my "friends" are now incarcerated or dead by their own hands. Today, I am aware that I am the end result of God's grace and mercy because I was headed in the same direction as my friends. I could have suffered the same tragic end as they did.

My mother suffered greatly because of my father's abuse. In

truth, she was in a desperate state of mind when she found herself alone and with two young children to raise. She had to work three jobs. She used to be one of those people who claimed to be a Christian, but in her own way, while searching for answers in witchcraft and Santeria.

While she searched for those answers, I was consumed with depression. I was enraged and felt great pain in my heart, to such a degree, that I came close to killing a person and managed to inflict a lot of pain to others. I reached the point of wanting out; I contemplated suicide.

For years people would talk to me about Christ, but I continually rejected Him because I thought that receiving Jesus in my heart was worthless. However, one day, tired of the filth that surrounded my life, I fell to my knees in my room and cried out to God. I had never cried so much in my life, not even when my grandfather died. At that moment, while I was kneeling, I said to God, "If you are real, I beg you to save my life." At that moment, I received Jesus in my heart and the next day I went to church. God filled the void that was in my heart. I found in Him the love that I had been missing my entire life.

I realize that I am a walking miracle because my life was totally transformed. Now, after knowing Jesus, I am the happiest man alive because He is in my life. I have the peace and love that cannot be found in any drug, friend, gang, or woman.

My encounter with Jesus was so powerful, that although I was only 16, I left in one day everything that I knew, to serve Him. I got so crazy that I practically won my whole school for Christ.

Today, I am a man of prayer. I follow the example of Jesus, who being also God, had to pray. If Jesus had to spend hours in prayer, then I must also pray for hours because I recognize that I cannot do anything in my own strength. I depend totally on Him. Prayer is the instrument, the way that God uses to help us develop our faith. Prayer helps us to depend on Him for everything. Through prayer, we learn what God's perfect will and purpose is for our lives and what plans He wants us to complete during our stay on earth.

A man who does not pray is dry inside, dead spiritually; he is like a man who does not breath for there is no breath left in him. God's life is not in him.

I am now 21 years old and I am happy to say that the early morning prayer, on my knees, changed my life. Prayer is not a waste of time. What do we accomplish through prayer? Prayer helps us to save time rather than to waste it while we try to do things in our own strength. Through prayer, we will reach our destiny, but without prayer, we delay the plans of God for our lives.

I knew that I had the spirit of warfare in me, but everytime I fought, I did it in my own crazy way. This is why I am eternally thankful to Pastor Ana Maldonado because through her, my prayer life changed; she taught me to pray. Now that I have learned to pray strategically and effectively, I see radical changes take place in my personal and devotional life. When the war is great, the level of authority increases and consequently the sanctity in our lives must also increase. We must keep our heart and every area of our lives in check because that is where many of us lose the war.

I have learned, with Pastor Ana Maldonado, not to be passive against the forces of darkness. People lose the war while they sleep. She has a particular boldness to confront the kingdom of darkness without fear of the devil. She lives with that kind of attitude all the time. I have learned to take by force from the spirit realm everything that belongs to me. But above all things, I have learned from her to love and to fear God. Now, we both share in her passion to destroy the works of the devil and to establish the Kingdom of God on earth.

We cannot enter into war until we learn to pray. We cannot make war unless we have a lifestyle of prayer and worship. It is during those times of intimacy with the Lord that we learn to be guided by the Holy Spirit to do warfare. Wars are never fought in human strength but with the power of the Holy Spirit. This is why the Word of God says, *"For we do not know what we should pray for as we ought."*

The hardest war that I have won through prayer was the war of criticism and man's opinion of others. Whenever we want to do something for God, the enemy tries to oppose it, wanting to give his opinion and causing fear. But that is precisely the time when we should hold on to God and obey Him, not man. I understand that rejection, persecution, and fear of being criticized are wars that I have fought with all that is in me and which I have won through perseverance. God has given me the victory and I know that the enemy has been confronted. Now, I am free and I know where I am going with Jesus!

I strongly believe that this book will revolutionize, transform, and cause a revival and an awakening in God's people. It will encourage those who believe that without prayer or spiritual warfare they can accomplish what God has entrusted them to do, to pray and to depend on God. Pastor Ana Maldonado is the living testimony of a woman who confronts the enemy face to face, everyday, in prayer and warfare. We are witnesses of God's support and the powerful results of her faithful prayer.

"All good things are worth fighting for"

Lizandro Parra

The first time I heard of Jesus I was 25 years old. At that time, I prayed the sinner's prayer only to satisfy the person who had invited me to church, but it was that small prayer that allowed the Holy Spirit to enter my life. For some time, I tried to walk away from sin and to walk the right path. Unfortunately, the addictions, money, the pleasures of this world, and lust led me down the wrong path. I fell so deep into the things of the world that it took me 15 years after that first encounter with Jesus to return to Him; I was ruined, destroyed, and on the brink of death. Seven years before my reconciliation with the Lord, I had a dream that showed me a set of feet; I kept seeing those feet save me over and over again from the continuous attacks of the devil; they helped me to understand the power in His name and the power of His blood. Praise God, that dream became a reality!

Today, I am a living, breathing testimony of what the powerful hand of God can do for one person; He saved me from certain death, from being imprisoned, from wickedness, from losing myself, and from a work of witchcraft that almost destroyed my health and my life.

When my relationship with the Lord was restored, the conviction of sin in my life was so powerful that I used to feel the need to pray the sinner's prayer over and over again. It was such a wonderful relief for me to realize that the only friend who was still with me from the days of abundance, sin, and corruption, was Jesus of Nazareth; He was the only one who gave me a hand when all others deserted me.

I started to serve God with all my heart in the worship ministry. However, when I arrived at El Rey Jesus, I understood that I was a Christian on fire, but without knowledge. I had no idea how to pray, and my gifts, the ones given to me by the Lord, were dormant and I did not know how to activate them.

I am thankful for Pastors Guillermo and Ana Maldonado because through their teachings I received inspiration and strength to grow. Through Pastor Ana Maldonado, I was trained on the battlefield. When I joined the early morning prayer team, I felt ashamed because I was the only man in the group who did not know how to pray. When I noticed that most of the people were women, I did not want to return because of my "macho" attitude and my judgmental predisposition. I remember one morning when Pastor Ana asked a short and slender young woman (Dianita) to pray. My immediate thought was, "Ha! The devil is going to eat her alive," but when she opened her mouth to pray, the power, authority, and boldness that came from her mouth took me by surprise; I had to kneel and ask God to forgive me.

Today I recognize the great power that women of God have when they pray. It was through prayer that the Lord delivered me from that "macho" spirit, from bondage, and strongholds of darkness that tormented me as a result of the "easy" and corrupt life that I lived in the past. Thanks to prayer, I was delivered from bondage, including my "excessive love" for the worship ministry. I also learned to love Jesus as first in my life and to prepare for my true calling, that of an evangelist.

Living a lifestyle of prayer taught me to submit to my pastor's authority. It also gave me the victory of seeing, feeling, and hearing what I was unable to see, hear, and feel before. Before the discipline of prayer, I was a Christian open to the enemy's attacks, but now I can declare that I am a man of prayer and a Christian who knows how to fight for the lost souls, your family, and your ministry. Before, the devil did with me as he pleased, but now I tell the devil, "Prepare yourself because I will destroy you before you take one step towards me."

Just as I am able to recognize the power of God in women of prayer, I am also able to tell the men who do not pray to stop their lazy and weak attitude. It was hard for me to begin to pray, but because of Pastor Ana's constant challenge to the men to pray, I understood that I had to learn to fight in the spirit realm in the same way that I would do it in the natural if someone were to mess with my wife and children. I also learned to assume my position of high priest or spiritual leader in my home. Today, I am able to say that a man who prays and who stands firm, delivers lethal blows to the enemy. The devil wants men to feel worthless, thus he tries to seduce them into watching more television; he tries to make them busy in other things, in order to prevent them from spending time in prayer.

I know that perseverance, continuity, and righteous living are ingredients needed for success in any area of ministry. Many men are experiencing spiritual, physical, and financial poverty because they have never chosen to make themselves worthy; to be firm and strong and to pray. I can testify that when a man begins to pray, God lifts him up spiritually, financially, and morally; also, God gives him grace and favor before men. A real man is not a controlling "macho" man who loves to scream at women; a real man knows how to groan, moan, wail, and cry in God's presence.

Getting out from Satan's grip and totally surrendering to the Lord and to the power of prayer took 15 years to accomplish. In those 15 years, I came close to losing my life and my salvation. For this reason, I understand that knowing Jesus and inviting Him into my life was the best decision of my life and the best thing that could have happened to me! You have a powerful weapon in your hands called *From Prayer to Warfare*, do not wait any longer; begin to pray today!

"Use your authority; kick the devil out of your house and your life and make him repay you seven times what he stole from you!"

Dear friend: If you want to receive the gift of eternal life and share in the move of God on earth but you have never acknowledged that Jesus Christ is the Son of God, who died and suffered for your sins at the cross, you can do it right now. Please join me in repeating the following prayer of repentance out loud.

The Sinner's Prayer

"Heavenly Father, I recognize that I am a sinner and that my sin separates me from you. Right now, of my own free will, I repent from all of my sins and confess Jesus as my Lord and Savior. I believe that Jesus died for my sins. I believe, with all my heart, that God the Father raised Him from the dead. Jesus, I ask you to come into my heart and change my life. I renounce all covenants that I made with the enemy. If I die right now, when I open my eyes, I will be in your arms. Amen!

If this prayer reflects the sincere desire of your heart, observe what Jesus said about the decision you just made:

> *"⁹If you confess with your mouth the Lord Jesus and believe in your heart that God has raised Him from the dead, you will be saved. ¹⁰For with the heart one believes unto righteousness and with the mouth confession is made unto salvation."*
> *Romans 10.9, 10*
>
> *"⁴⁷Most assuredly, I say to you, he who believes in Me has everlasting life." John 6.47*

Dear Internet user ...

The Sinner's Prayer

Bibliography

Biblia de Estudio Arco Iris. Version Reina-Valera, Revision 1960, Biblical Text copyright© 1960, Sociedades Bíblicas in Latin America, Nashville, Tennessee, ISBN: 1-55819-555-6.

Biblia Plenitud. Version Reina-Valera, Revision 1960, ISBN: 089922279X, Caribe Editorial, Miami, Florida.

Diccionario Español a Inglés, Inglés a Español. Larousse Editorial S.A., printed in Dinamarca, Num. 81, México, ISBN: 2034202007, ISBN: 70607371X , 1993.

El Pequeño Larousse Ilustrado. 2002 Spes Editorial, S.L. Barcelona; Editions Larousse, S.A. de C.V. México, D.F., ISBN: 970-22-0020-2.

Expanded Edition the Amplified Bible. Zondervan Bible Publishers. ISBN: 0310951682, 1987 – Lockman Foundation USA.

Reina-Valera 1995 - Edición de Estudio, (United States of America: Sociedades Bíblicas Unidas) 1998.

Strong James, LL.D, S.T.D., *Concordancia Strong Exhaustiva de la Biblia*, Caribe Editorial, Inc., Thomas Nelson, Inc., Publishers, Nashville, TN - Miami, FL, USA., 2002. ISBN: 0-89922-382-6.

The New American Standard Version. Zordervan Publishing Company, ISBN: 0310903335.

The Tormont Webster's Illustrated Encyclopedic Dictionary. ©1990 Tormont Publications.

Vine, W.E. *Diccionario Expositivo de las Palabras del Antiguo Testamento y Nuevo Testamento.* Caribe Editorial, Inc./Division Thomas Nelson, Inc., Nashville, TN, ISBN: 0899224954, 1999.

Ward, Lock A. *Nuevo Diccionario de la Biblia.* Unilit Editorial: Miami, Florida, ISBN: 07899-0217-6, 1999.

PUBLICATIONS

LEADERS THAT CONQUER

Guillermo Maldonado

Learn to overcome every limitation set before you. Change your life as you inspire and motivate those who follow after you as you become a leader that conquers!

ISBN: 1-59272-023-4 | 206 pgs.

INNER HEALING AND DELIVERANCE

Guillermo Maldonado

This book will help you to understand the areas in your life that need to be dealt with; only our Lord and His revealed truth can make you totally free.

ISBN: 1-59272-007-2 | 269 pp.

THE HOLY ANOINTING

Guillermo Maldonado

This book provides basic principles for ministering in the anointing which is the manifestation of the Holy Spirit. When we learn to operate under the anointing, we become effective ministers who will witness supernatural results, not only in ministry, but in every day life.

ISBN: 1-59272-038-2 | 158 pp.

OVERCOMING DEPRESSION

Guillermo Maldonado

This book, written in line with God's Word is the perfect, practical, step-by-step guide on how to overcome depression for-ever!

ISBN: 1-59272-041-2 | 68 pgs.

DISCOVER YOUR PURPOSE AND CALLING IN GOD

Guillermo Maldonado

Have you ever wondered why you were created? Did you know that God gave you gifts that will bless you and the world around you? Learn the answers to these ques-tions, and learn God's purpose and calling for your life - today!

ISBN: 1-59272-094-3

FORGIVENESS

Guillermo Maldonado

It is impossible to avoid being offended. At some point in your life, you must choose to forgive those who hurt you.

ISBN: 1-59272-040-4 | 76 pgs.

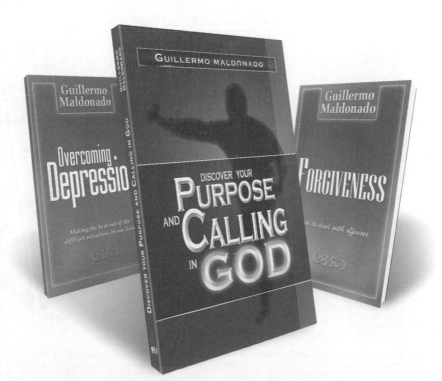

PUBLICATIONS

SUPERNATURAL EVANGELISM

Guillermo Maldonado

This book will challenge you to win souls for Christ; it gives you practical teaching on how to present God's powerful message of salvation!

ISBN: 1-59272-088-9 | 134 pgs.

BIBLICAL FOUNDATIONS FOR A NEW BELIEVER

Guillermo Maldonado

The biblical foundation found in this book will guide your first steps as you experience your new life as a born-again believer; it will help you to grow and understand every step of your new journey in Christ.

ISBN: 1-59272-089-7 | 96 pgs.

THE FAMILY

Guillermo Maldonado

What are your responsibilities? Do you know how to communicate effectively? Are you single and satisfied? What about your children? This book will answer every question you ever had about marriage and the family.

ISBN: 1-59272-089-0 | 162 pgs.

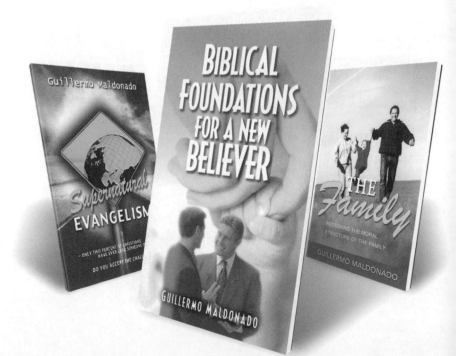

SPIRITUAL MATURITY

Guillermo Maldonado

Learn to identify the different levels of spiritual maturity. What level are you in?

ISBN: 1-59272-092-7

THE NEW WINE GENERATION

Guillermo Maldonado

The New Wine generation, under the anointing and the power of the Holy Spirit, must conquer and take back what the enemy has stolen. This book will instruct and inspire you to walk in the spiritual realm and to destroy all works of evil.

ISBN: 1-59272-039-0 | 195 pgs.

HOW TO HEAR THE VOICE OF GOD

Guillermo Maldonado

Would you like to learn how to hear God's voice? After you read this book you will be able to discern God's voice, and you will learn how to walk in the supernatural will of God.

ISBN: 1-59272-091-9 | 156 pgs.

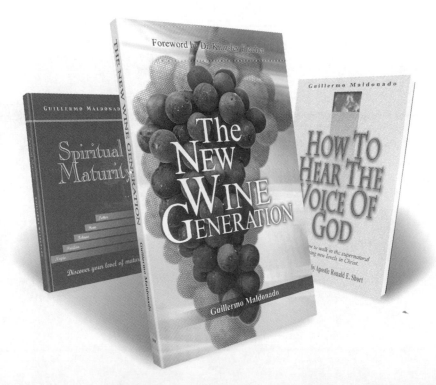

HOW TO RETURN TO OUR FIRST LOVE

Guillermo Maldonado

This wonderful book will take you back to the fire that burned in your spirit when you first met Christ. It will help you to understand what caused its flames to diminish. It will teach you how to breathe life back into your spirit, and renew your relationship with our precious Lord.

ISBN: 1-59272-062-1

PRAYER

Guillermo Maldonado

Breathe life back into your prayer life. Learn how to go into deeper levels of prayer as you develop a close and intimate relationship with God. This book will help you to succeed in your ministry and in all facets of life.

ISBN: 1-59272-090-0 | 180 pgs.

THE CHARACTER OF A LEADER

Guillermo Maldonado

The solid foundation of a ministry depends on the character of the individual. If we have problems with our character, these will eventually destroy us. Therefore, let us learn from His Word what we have to do for God to shape our character.

ISBN: 1-59272-061-3

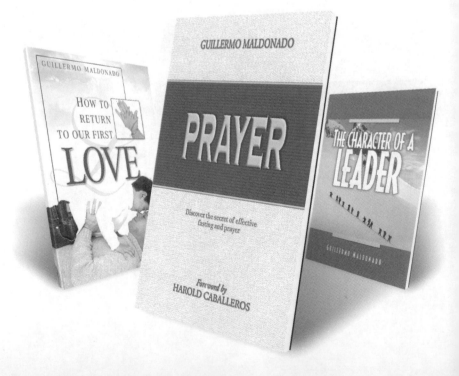